McKinsey Quarterly

On the cover: Competing for Asia's consu P9-CCK-320

2009
Number 4

This Quarter:
Has Asia's moment come?

Dominic Barton

Think regionally, act locally: Four steps to reaching the Asian consumer

Todd Guild

A consumer paradigm for China

Janamitra Devan,
Micah Rowland, and
Jonathan Woetzel

Feature article

Strategy

Leadership lessons for hard times

Dennis Carey,
Michael Patsalos-Fox,
and Michael Useem

Equally as important as understanding the mistakes that sparked the financial and economic crisis is knowing how to lead a company through the resultant tough times. To contribute to the discussion, we interviewed the leaders of 14 major companies, asking them to reflect on what they felt they had learned.

The companies these CEOs, chairmen, and presidents lead are all in diverse industries, face varied challenges, and have performed quite differently. What emerges from the interviews is agreement on some broad principles that can help guide behavior in the executive suite and in the boardroom, as well as interactions with employees, customers, and investors.

This article contains the following sidebar:
Leaders coping with crisis:
Selected McKinsey
Global Survey Results

Special report

Corporate Finance + By Invitation

How sustainability programs create value

Valuing social responsibility programs

Sheila Bonini,
Timothy M. Koller, and
Philip H. Mirvis

Executives struggling to cut costs may be skeptical about implementing and sustaining environmental, social, and governance programs, at least without clear data demonstrating their financial benefits.

Yet many companies are creating real value through their ESG activities—through increased sales, decreased costs, or reduced risks. In this article, the authors identify programs that make real contributions to the bottom line in a way that's already assessed by the market—growth, return on capital, risk management, and quality of management.

When sustainability means more than green

Adam Werbach

Society is increasingly holding global businesses accountable as the only institutions strong enough to meet the huge long-term challenges facing our planet. Companies must develop and execute a strategy for sustainability—one that takes into account every dimension of the business environment: social, economic, and cultural, as well as natural.

Imagined and implemented fully, sustainability drives a bottom-line strategy to save costs, a top-line strategy to reach a new consumer base, and a talent strategy to get, keep, and develop creative employees. The stories of two companies show how these ideas play out in actual organizations.

Interview

High Tech

**McKinsey conversations
with global leaders:**
John Chambers of Cisco
Systems

James Manyika

Special report

Energy, Resources, Materials

China + US: Collaborating on clean energy

China and the US:
The potential of
a clean-tech partnership

Jonathan Woetzel

4

Correction: In *McKinsey Quarterly,* 2009 Number 3, we incorrectly identified the
authors of "Strategic planning in a crisis" as Andrew Cheung, Eric Kutcher,
and Dilip Wagle. The actual authors are Renée Dye, Olivier Sibony, and S. Patrick
Viguerie. We sincerely regret the error.

Editorial

Board of Editors
Allan R. Gold, *Editor-in-Chief*
Bill Javetski
Tom Kiely
Allen P. Webb

Senior Editors
Thomas Fleming
Lars Föyen
Roger Malone
Dennis Swinford

Associate Editors
Lillian Cunningham
Heather Ploog
Mary Reddy, *Information Design*
David Sims, *mckinseyquarterly.com*

***McKinsey Quarterly* Fellow**
Mrinalini Reddy

Editorial and Design Production
Donald Bergh, *Design Director*
Sue Rini, *Managing Editor*
Roger Draper, *Copy Chief*
Drew Holzfeind, *Assistant Managing Editor*
Delilah Zak, *Associate Design Director*
Veronica Belsuzarri, *Senior Designer*
Andrew Cha, *Web Production Assistant*

Editorial Surveys
Josselyn Simpson
Martin Rouse
Karina Lacouture

***McKinsey Quarterly* China**
Gary Chen, *Editor*
Min Ma, *Assistant Managing Editor*
Melody Xie, *Production Assistant*

Business

Jeff Pundyk, *Publisher*
Sammy Pau, *Finance*
Debra Petritsch, *Logistics*
Pamela Kelly, *Customer Service Coordinator*

Digital Media
Nicole Adams
Devin A. Brown
Jennifer Orme
Jim Santo

Web sites
mckinseyquarterly.com
china.mckinseyquarterly.com

E-mail
info@mckinseyquarterly.com

How to change your mailing address:
McKinsey clients via e-mail
updates@mckinseyquarterly.com

Premium members via Web site
mckinseyquarterly.com/my_profile.aspx

McKinsey alumni via e-mail
alumni_relations@mckinsey.com

How to contact the *Quarterly*:
E-mail customer service
info@mckinseyquarterly.com

To request permission to republish an article
quarterly_reprints@mckinsey.com

To comment on an article
quarterly_comments@mckinsey.com

On Our Web Site

Now available on mckinseyquarterly.com

Interactives

Evaluating the potential of solar technologies

This interactive offers a snapshot of the leading contenders in solar technology and evaluates the advantages and long-term economic potential of each—as well as the likely challenges ahead.

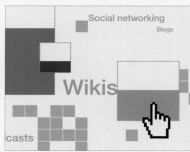

Business and Web 2.0: An interactive feature

Explore, track, and customize three years of survey results on how businesses use new Web technologies and tools.

Enduring Ideas: The business system

A McKinsey alumnus describes how companies can use the business system to evaluate their choices at each stage in the process of creating and delivering products. Aligning conduct at every step with the company's value proposition creates a truly integrated business strategy.

Articles

How to optimize knowledge sharing in a factory network

Designing a manufacturing network entails devising and managing flows of innovation and know-how—not just determining what to produce and where—and organizing the resulting logistics flows.

Unlocking the potential of frontline managers

Instead of administrative work and meetings, they should focus on coaching their employees and on constantly improving quality.

IT architecture: Cutting costs and complexity

A joint effort by IT and business leaders can help companies not only to save money but also to prepare for the return of growth.

Rethinking the model for offshoring services

BPO providers often rely on a limited number of geographic locations, exposing themselves to unnecessary risk. They can mitigate these risks in the same way that financial managers do—by diversifying their holdings.

Conversation starter

What shape will the wireless Web take?

The era of the nomadic Web is upon us. But questions still remain as to how things will actually play out in a wireless world.

Surveys

Unprepared for changes in health care: McKinsey Global Survey Results

Ongoing health care reform and a new economic environment will have a significant impact on the industry. Yet most players are not ready for change. Those who are innovate differently and focus on increasing the value of health care.

Put our headlines on your page

Our widgets let you share the latest *Quarterly* headlines on your social network, blog, or personalized page. Show all headlines or just those for a single function. **mckinseyquarterly.com/widgets**

More from McKinsey

Join the conversation on What Matters

Join this discussion at: **whatmatters.mckinseydigital.com**

McKinsey's *What Matters* convenes leading thinkers from around the world weighing in on topics from geopolitics to the credit crisis to health care that will shape our future. In our latest install-ment, experts debate whether consumers will pay for content online—and the implications for Internet business models.

Video and audio podcasts on iTunes

Download conversations with executives and authors in audio or video from iTunes. **mckinseyquarterly.com/itunes**

Recent podcast:
Deriving value from Web 2.0

Join the *McKinsey Quarterly* community on Facebook

facebook.com/mckinseyquarterly

Follow us on Twitter

Receive notification of new articles by following **@McKQuarterly** on Twitter.

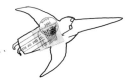

Letters to the Editor

Reader responses to articles in *McKinsey Quarterly*, 2009 Number 3

Rebuilding corporate reputations

A perfect storm has hit the standing of big business. Companies must step up their reputation-management efforts in response.

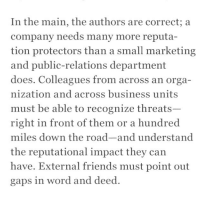

In the main, the authors are correct; a company needs many more reputation protectors than a small marketing and public-relations department does. Colleagues from across an organization and across business units must be able to recognize threats—right in front of them or a hundred miles down the road—and understand the reputational impact they can have. External friends must point out gaps in word and deed.

But one of the article's fundamental assumptions doesn't account for a very real and very active threat to reputation: the motivated adversary. The authors write much about "getting your side of the story out" and spreading "positive messages" when confronted with reputational threats, particularly in the media. The assumption here is that a company can meet serious, if not legitimate, criticisms by simply proclaiming, "Yeah, but look at all the good stuff we're doing!" It also assumes that ardent critics have open minds and can be persuaded. More often than not, this just isn't the case.

No amount of positive messaging is going to pacify those with entrenched and principled disagreements with a company's actions. Advocacy organizations dedicated to organic food and healthful eating simply aren't going to be on board with Fast Food Chain X. Greenpeace will not be persuaded that Oil Company Y is good for the environment.

Where companies can discredit critics, they should. Where there is a legitimate deficiency outed, companies should fix it. Over time, doing the right thing—and communicating it authentically—wins friends.

"Getting positive messages out" doesn't. Wal-Mart, as an example, was long a favorite target of environmental-activist groups. Recognizing that it could do better, Wal-Mart stepped up its game, made a real commitment to sustainability, communicated it effectively, and now stands among the world's enterprise leaders in responsible environmental stewardship.

Winning hearts and minds is nice, but not always in the cards. Sometimes, getting an opponent to leave you alone is the most prudent course of action—and yields the best outcome.

Mike Sacks
Communications consultant,
MWW Group
New York, NY USA

Let's remember that building trust is a mind-set, not a management exercise. Note well the Johnson & Johnson credo and the way it is used to elicit behaviors of trust in employees and other stakeholders. From the CEO on down, all do sing from the same hymnal. The process can work.

David Frank
Managing director,
MEDx Associates
Springfield, NJ USA

A strong corporate reputation is based entirely on stakeholder trust. Weak management tends to assume that negative information about their organizations will be overvalued and positive information will be undervalued, so the best policy is minimal information. That makes them untrustworthy, and their prophecy becomes self-fulfilling. Strong managements assume that all information ultimately will be properly valued and that their job is to perform in a way that maximizes the share of positive information. That makes them trustworthy sources, with equally self-fulfilling results.

Wayne Buckhout
Senior vice president,
CTC Investor Relations
Dayton, OH USA

I am surprised that you do not mention advertising as a key way to build reputation. People respond to public, paid-for messages and are influenced by them. Advertising is the basis of the free press in democracy. Ignoring its influence in helping to shape reputation is naive.

Lou Rubin
Director,
The Gate Worldwide
New York, NY USA

The consumer decision journey

Consumers are moving outside the purchasing funnel—changing the way they research and buy your products. If your marketing hasn't changed in response, it should.

The key word in this piece is *influence*. And not just at the time of purchase but as the consumer begins to filter the brand options. I appreciate the funnel and circular-journey comparisons and believe that the process has always been circular. The funnel suggests that the process ends, but if the consumer does not enjoy the brand and quits it, that does not mean that the contact never happened. Perhaps the consumer told fellow consumers about the bad experience or, for years to follow, that consumer carried their less-than-positive reaction to the brand when they subsequently ran into it—each action suggesting a relationship of sorts.

This is a great paper, but what requires more emphasis is the fact that in recent years consumers have progressively migrated to trusting friends and family more than institutions (government, religion, associations). That peer-to-peer influence, now turbocharged by social media, is largely the driver of what

we at DDB call "swarm marketing." This is differentiated from traditional marketing and advertising that merely broadcasts to large groups of people and hopes that a few will accept the proposition. Swarm marketing accepts that people are homogeneous beings and like to belong to groups with similar values, attributes, and goals. Once you recognize those groups and the influencers within them, it is the goal of brand communications to present an honest, authentic, differentiated, and engaging brand. This will invite consumers into the circular process but will not guarantee their loyalty. And that is what makes brands and branding great—they are all about choice, and that choice is in the hands of each individual consumer.

Jeff Swystun
Chief communications officer,
DDB Worldwide
New York, NY USA

More letters from our readers on these and other articles are available on mckinseyquarterly.com.

In Brief

Research and perspectives on management

Conversation Starter

Short essays by leading thinkers on management topics

'Power curves': What natural and economic disasters have in common

Michele Zanini

Executives, strategists, and economic forecasters, somewhat sheepish after missing the "big one"—last year's global credit crisis—turned to the lexicon of natural disasters, describing the shock as a tsunami hitting markets and as an earthquake shaking the world economy's foundations. Shopworn as these metaphors may be, they aptly capture the extreme and unexpected nature of the circumstances. In fact, the parallels between the dynamics and failures of man-made systems, such as the economy or the electricity grid, and similarly complex natural ones are bringing new ideas to economic forecasting, strategic planning, and risk management. This trend may have profound implications for policy makers, economists, and corporate strategists alike.

Scientists, sometimes in cooperation with economists, are taking the lead in a young field that applies complexity theory to economic research, rejecting the traditional view of the economy as a fully transparent, rational system striving toward equilibrium. The statistical physics professor and earthquake authority Didier Sornette, for example, leads the Financial Crisis Observatory, in Zurich, which uses concepts and mathematical models that draw on complexity theory and statistical physics to understand financial bubbles and economic crises.

Sornette aims to predict extreme outcomes in complex systems. Many other scientists in the field of complexity theory argue that earthquakes, forest fires, power blackouts, and

Michele Zanini is an associate principal in McKinsey's Boston office.

the like are extremely difficult or even impossible to foresee because they are the products of many interdependent "agents" and cascades of events in inherently unstable systems that generate large variations. One symptom of such a system's behavior is that the frequency and magnitude of outcomes can be described by a mathematical relationship called a "power law," characterized by a short "head" of frequently occurring small events, dropping off to a long "tail" of increasingly rare but much larger ones.

The power law phenomenon, explored in recent bestselling books and observed by academics for decades, seems to be applicable to a wide range of currently relevant economic outcomes, including financial crises, industrial production, and corporate bankruptcies.

If, for instance, you plot the frequency of banking crises around the world from 1970 to 2007, as well as their magnitude as measured by four-year losses of GDP for each affected country, you get a typical power curve

Exhibit: **The banking crisis power curve**
Plotting the frequency and magnitude of banking crises creates a typical power curve. This example compares the bank crisis power curve with that of earthquakes.

Number of worldwide banking crises, 1970–2007

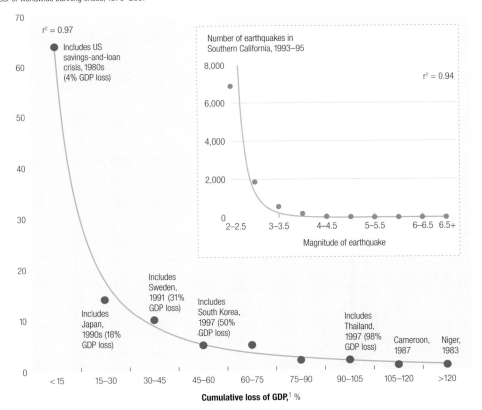

r^2 is the proportion of variance explained by a regression.

[1]IMF economists computed GDP loss by extrapolating real GDP from pre-crisis trend and adding the yearly percentage difference between actual GDP and extrapolated GDP for first 4 years of crisis (for more details, see Luc Laeven and Fabian Valencia, *Systemic Banking Crises: A New Database*, IMF working paper, November 2008).

Source: International Monetary Fund (IMF); US Geological Survey; McKinsey analysis

pattern, with a short head of almost 70 crises, each with accumulated losses of less than 15 percent of GDP, quickly falling off to a long tail of very few—but massive—crises (exhibit). While the most extreme cases involve smaller, less developed countries, the same distribution also applies to more developed ones—and with much larger absolute values for GDP loss. Earthquakes, forest fires, and blackouts yield a similar power curve pattern—for instance, from 1993 to 1995, Southern California registered 7,000 tremors at 2.0–2.5 on the Richter scale, falling off to the 1994 Northridge earthquake, at the end of the tail, with a magnitude of 6.7. This suggests that the economy, like other complex systems characterized by power law behavior, is inherently unstable and prone to occasional huge failures. Intriguing stuff, but how can corporate strategists, economists, and policy makers use it?

Make the system the unit of analysis. You can't assess the behavior and performance of a specific agent—for example, a financial-services company—without gauging the behavior and performance of the system in which it is embedded.

Don't assume stability and do take a long look back. Major systemic imbalances and corrections are highly likely, and everyone should be wary of new economic paradigms to the contrary. It's equally important to take a truly historical perspective and consider a system's underlying patterns. If you look at the sharp rise in US corporate profits from 1997 to 2007 in isolation, it might seem like steady, sustainable development that can be justified by pointing to near-term trends, such as globalization and productivity growth. Yet it becomes a striking departure from the historical norm when you look back and find that profits last hit such a lofty percentage of GDP more than 50 years ago and dropped shortly thereafter. Outliers such as these should not be ignored but rather studied closely for clues that might help us understand current and future events.

Read what other people are saying at mckinseyquarterly.com, then join the conversation.

In our economic system, new technologies mean interactions are getting more frequent, more cost-efficient, and faster. But will an increased volume of interaction make future economic cycles even more pronounced? Or might the increasing speeds of interaction have a 'dampening' effect on these cycles, or perhaps make the swings between them shorter in duration?

—Don Peppers

How does one know if one is on a 'power curve'? Most of the above instances were obvious in retrospect, but weren't apparent until it was too late. Early warning signs almost always get dismissed. For example, Lehman credit default swaps pointed to a serious problem long before the company went under. Obvious in hindsight, but not that clear in the moment.

—Sara Mathew

Focus on early warning. The inherent uncertainty of complex systems makes point predictions unreliable. Much as earthquake scientists are developing tsunami early-warning systems, corporate strategists should monitor potential indications that economic stress might be building in their industries. One indicator could be changes in the exit and entry rates in a particular industry. It's notable, for instance, that specialized US mortgage companies experienced difficulties in late 2006 and that several went bankrupt long before the problems spread to financial institutions with a strong mortgage exposure and then to broader financial institutions and other major companies.

Build flexible business models. Corporate leaders might consider robust business models incorporating some slack and flexibility instead of the models most common today, which aim to optimize value in the most likely future scenario and thus leave companies exposed when conditions change dramatically.

The offshoring of production or services to a number of continents and countries, for example, is surely more costly, under stable conditions, than maintaining a single center but would protect a company in the event of an unexpected regional or national economic crisis.

Learn from scientists studying other complex systems. Strategists, economists, and others should consider several other potential parallels. To take one example, what economic-policy lessons could be drawn from the observation that efforts to put out small forest fires quickly may in time lead to large-scale fires, because the rapid mitigation of small ones allows burnable undergrowth to accumulate? o

Copyright © 2009 McKinsey & Company. All rights reserved.

We welcome your comments on these articles. Please send them to quarterly_comments@ mckinsey.com.

It is meaningless to talk about a 'typical' event that follows the power law. For this reason, they are best plotted on log-log scales. The lack of a single, dominating scale makes it difficult to deal intuitively with these events. Some power distributions cannot be handled easily by statistics. All this hinders our understanding and requires much more reliance on math and modeling, which are often imperfect.

—*Slav Hermanowicz*

Interesting that there suddenly is more and more discussion on 'outliers' after the economic crisis. I wonder if the bell curve will once again become 'counter thinking' in 5 years time after everybody is looking for the next big 'outlier' event.

This article is thought provoking as we look for patterns from other fields to see if somehow we can predict events like these or even estimate the scale of the event.

—*Kannan Gopalakrishnan*

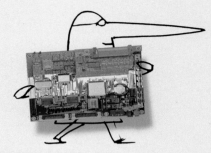

Strengthening India's offshoring industry

Noshir Kaka

The global economic downturn has slowed the growth of India's technology and business services industry, but beyond the current crisis the industry faces a changing global environment that will probably cut into the country's worldwide market share. McKinsey analysis suggests that there is little immediate risk to India's dominance of the market for offshore technology and business services. But the country's share could sink to 40 percent by 2020, from more than 50 percent at the end of 2008, primarily as a result of increased competition from other countries, talent and infrastructure constraints, and an unhelpful regulatory environment. But changes in the global market could also give India opportunities, especially if its companies become more innovative and rely less on low labor costs.

The revenues of India's business and technology services companies have grown to about $58 billion at the end of 2008 (including about $46 billion in exports), from $4 billion in 1998. McKinsey expects the global market for offshore business and technology services to grow to about $500 billion by 2020, from the current $80 billion a year.

Noshir Kaka is a director in McKinsey's Mumbai office.

Several factors will contribute to this global growth. Core markets— for instance, large financial-services and telecommunications companies in developed economies—should continue to expand along with the global economy, once growth returns. The pace of growth could slow down, however, if processes are automated and standardized more quickly than seems likely now. Corporate budget cuts during the downturn and protectionist regulation could also dampen demand from core and other markets.

Much of the industry's expansion will come from increased demand from emerging markets (primarily China and India, but also Brazil and Russia) and other nontraditional customers. Individuals and small and midsize enterprises will find it easier to use offshore services as communications technologies advance, costs go down, and business models evolve. Finally, new kinds of customers—particularly in the public sector (including state-owned enterprises), as well as health care providers—will likely turn to outsourced business and technology services.

But as the pie expands, India will be hard pressed to maintain its market share unless its providers become more innovative and global.

First, the industry faces domestic constraints. India produces too few suitable university graduates a year to maintain its market share. Strained transportation systems and power and water supplies in the country's leading cities, including offshoring hubs such as Hyderabad and Chennai, will also hinder the industry's expansion.

Another problem for India is that everyone wants to join the party. China, Egypt, many Eastern European countries, and dozens of others are fighting aggressively to build their domestic business and technology services industries, offering tax benefits and improved infrastructure as incentives. Egypt, for example, is developing university programs intended to provide the industry with 32,000 employable graduates by 2010.

Finally, government policies—which have over the years supported the industry—have become less favorable in recent times. At present, extending the government's fiscal incentives to the industry, for example, is decided on a year-to-year basis rather than as an integral part of a long-term policy. Meanwhile, the industry continues to be regulated by the Shops and Establishments Act and other laws not tailored to the service sector's requirements. Adding to the burden, these laws are applied inconsistently from state to state.

Indian business and technology services companies needn't stand by passively and watch their global market share decline. Innovation will be the key to maintaining and even expanding their market share. Business models that continue to focus on low labor costs won't suffice. Unfortunately, innovation isn't the industry's strong suit. The country still accounts for less than 1 percent of the patents issued

around the world annually. To address the opportunities in new geographic and industry markets and to serve individuals and small and midsize enterprises, business and technology services companies must create innovative products that address the needs of these new customers.

Areas that appear ripe include clinical research, mobile applications and platforms, and energy efficiency. Much as offshore companies remotely manage their customers' IT infrastructures, for example, they could remotely manage the energy consumed by their customers' air conditioning and heating systems. If successful, such efforts could contribute $100 billion to $130 billion in export revenues to India's offshoring industry by 2020, expanding its global market share to almost 60 percent.

Apart from an isolated failure in corporate governance, India's brand abroad has been burnished by the success of its technology and business services industry. But it will retain its luster and advantage over up-and-coming locations only by reinventing itself and looking beyond the low-cost labor model that served it well in the past. o

Copyright © 2009 McKinsey & Company. All rights reserved.

We welcome your comments on these articles. Please send them to quarterly_comments@ mckinsey.com.

Case in Point

When citizens are your customers

Sebastien Katch and Tim Morse

Situation

Any public-sector agency that directly interacts with large numbers of citizens often finds that demand for its services overwhelms the limited resources available to provide them. A government can't prioritize its citizen "customers" by using metrics like how valuable they are or how costly to serve—common practices in the private sector under similar circumstances. This was the problem facing a US federal agency seeking to make its call centers and paper-processing facilities more efficient. Rising budget pressure and demand for the agency's services had had the effect of compromising them. In fact, during times of peak demand, agents answered less than three-quarters of phone calls to the agency, which also processed less than half of all paper applications within its target response time.

Complication

Optimizing the resources allocated to the two channels proved difficult. The agency relied on a common pool of employees who switched between fielding calls and processing forms as necessary to meet spikes in demand. Yet the channels operated independently, with separate managers; the agency relied on personal relationships to exchange important information. What's more, pressure to respond immediately to phone calls often diverted agents from paper applications, unbalancing the two channels' service levels.

Resolution

The agency designed a labor allocation model around customer satisfaction ratings, creating "satisfaction curves" that revealed service breakpoints—levels at which delays made customer satisfaction drop significantly. In a mathematical model correlating the influence of a range of inputs on these satisfaction benchmarks, the agency set performance targets that reflected the breakpoints. That process helped managers to identify the trade-offs between staffing either channel optimally and satisfying customers in the other channel in real time, and therefore helped to improve the service balance between the two channels while also raising overall customer satisfaction. For the paper channel, the optimal allocation of resources called for a 20 to 30 percent increase in service delivery levels during periods of peak demand. Meanwhile, channel managers shared responsibility

Sebastien Katch is a consultant in McKinsey's Chicago office, and **Tim Morse** is a principal in the New Jersey office.

Exhibit: **Targeting satisfaction**

Definitions of service benchmarks can be based on customer-satisfaction breakpoints—levels at which delays cause customer satisfaction to drop significantly.

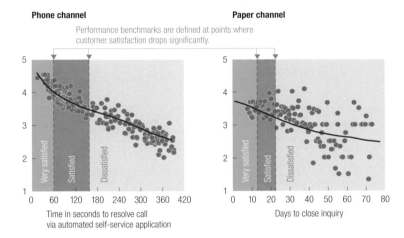

Average customer satisfaction score for US federal agency, on scale of 1 to 5, where 1 = very dissatisfied and 5 = very satisfied

Copyright © 2009 McKinsey & Company. All rights reserved.

We welcome your comments on these articles. Please send them to quarterly_comments@ mckinsey.com.

for generating and vetting the model's inputs—for instance, weekly projections of demand and operational assumptions about expected staffing levels.

Implications

With demand for services rising and budgets falling, governments around the world are under pressure to raise their game in service operations. By linking daily work to uncontroversial metrics (such as customer satisfaction ratings), public-sector organizations can improve their service levels and save money while honoring their universal-service obligation to treat all citizens equally. o

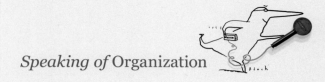

Speaking of Organization

An interview with Robert Sutton

Rik Kirkland

Layoffs, pay cuts, and organizational reordering have become widespread realities in the downturn. In this excerpt from a video interview (available on mckinseyquarterly.com), Robert Sutton, professor at the Stanford Graduate School of Engineering and noted author and specialist on management and organizations, offers his advice on how to be a good boss in today's difficult climate.

The *Quarterly*: *You did an article recently for the* Harvard Business Review, *"How to be a good boss in a bad economy." Frame the challenge for us.*

Robert Sutton: It's a combination of two things about power that are very well documented. One is that when people are in positions of power, for better or worse, they often become sort of oblivious to the needs and actions of the people who have less power than they do. And the other part of this "toxic tandem," a principle that I've stolen from a lot of good social psychologists, is sometimes called hypervigilance.

So if you think about the toxic tandem, you've got the boss, oblivious, and then the subordinates, even more and more worried. Bosses really have to keep in mind that there is a lot of research that shows that when people are looking at their boss and are worried about what their boss is doing, they tend to assume the worst. So little, tiny signals get magnified.

The *Quarterly*: *So what do you do?*

Robert Sutton: I see how hard this is on my various friends who are CEOs and how it just rips their guts out and how much they worry about it. But there is sort of a little recipe for being a good boss that actually goes back to some research I started in graduate school with my mentor, Robert Kahn, who is now, I think, 92 years old. The recipe is prediction, understanding, control, and compassion.

The idea of prediction is that if some sort of stress is coming through, it does much less damage to people when they know when they are safe versus when they are threatened. A good example of this comes from one of the CEOs I know—the head of a nonprofit. He was describing to me that things did not look good. His people were very nervous. So what he said to them was, "I promise you there will be no layoffs or pay cuts for 90 days; nothing is going to happen, so you're safe until then." So that is the

Rik Kirkland is McKinsey's director of publishing.

'The recipe for being a good boss is prediction, understanding, control, and compassion'

Robert Sutton
Professor, Stanford Graduate School of Engineering

kind of thing that gives people some bit of psychological safety. And also they know when to mobilize to worry about their lives.

The *Quarterly*: *So don't over-promise, but if you can at least give a certain window of stability, give it to them—right?*

Robert Sutton: Yes. So the next thing is understanding. It's very well documented that, independently of how stressful things are, human beings need to know why things happen. They need some sort of explanation. And there is sort of a challenge there, because if you give people too complicated an explana-tion, then they just get befuddled and freak out. There is an art to being able to give an explanation that's complicated but not *too* complicated, so they can follow it. Part of get-ting rid of the fear is having people understand it.

The next one is control—if you can give people some control over the way it happens. A good example of this, which I talk about in the article, occurred some years back. When A. G. Lafley came on in about 2000 as CEO of P&G, they still had John Pepper as the chair, and he described how they learned a lot about how to close plants. P&G used to sort of sneak out in

the middle of the night and do it. But they learned that when they announce the closing in advance, tell people why, give them all sorts of exit options and places where they can have control, and show com-passion that—and P&G has very good metrics—they end up keeping more good employees and getting better press in the community. And the other thing, which was quite important to them, is that sales of the company's products in the local community would not go down so much.

The *Quarterly*: *How do you deal with the folks who don't get laid off?*

Robert Sutton: When they see that it's fair, they are more likely to stay loyal, suffer less psychological damage, and also feel more guilty and work even harder to help you. There is actually this sort of weird, sneaky part of it, which is that if the survivors are treated well, they kind of feel guilty because of that "there but for the grace of God go I" sort of phenomenon. In fact, most of all the stuff I said about prediction, understanding, control, and compassion—whether people lose their jobs or not—has an effect on the whole system. **o**

Artwork by Serge Bloch/ Marlena Agency.

Copyright © 2009 McKinsey & Company. All rights reserved.

We welcome your com-ments on these articles. Please send them to quarterly_comments@ mckinsey.com.

To watch a video of the full interview, see 'Good boss, bad times,' on mckinseyquarterly.com.

Quarterly *Surveys*

Selected results from surveys of *McKinsey Quarterly*'s panel of global executives

Learning to cope with the crisis

A year after the global economic system nearly collapsed, many companies are finally finding ways to increase profits under the new economic conditions. But almost as many expect profits to continue falling; executives also indicate that their broader economic hopes remain fragile.

Copyright © 2009 McKinsey & Company. All rights reserved.

We welcome your comments on these articles. Please send them to quarterly_comments@mckinsey.com.

Executives are far more likely now to think that globalization will intensify than they were at the low point of the crisis. Five years from now, a much larger share of executives expect more integrated financial markets and more extensive global operations and international trade than expect the opposite. Forty-nine percent of respondents now expect greater financial-market integration; when we asked a similar question, in March 2009, only 35 percent did. Many expect more government involvement in economies and industries over the long term. o

The survey was conducted in September 2009 and includes the responses of 1,677 executives from around the world.

Exhibit: **Whither globalization?**

Thinking about trends related to globalization, what differences, if any, do you expect to see in the global economy over the next 5 years (through the end of 2014), compared with before September 2008?

% of respondents,[1] n = 1,677

Greater integration of financial markets	49	Decline in capital flows across countries	28
Decrease in commitment to free-market economics	44	Less movement of labor across national borders	24
Greater extent of companies' global operations	44	Less international trade	19
More international trade	42	Less integration of financial markets	17
Greater influence of international organizations	40	Increase in commitment to free-market economics	15
More movement of labor across national borders	35	Decline in extent of companies' global operations	15
Increase in capital flows across countries	32	Less influence of international organizations	13

[1]Respondents who answered "other" or "don't know" are not shown.

The full results of this survey, 'The crisis—one year on: McKinsey Global Economic Conditions Survey results,' are available on mckinseyquarterly.com/surveys.

On the cover:

Competing for Asia's consumers

Dinesh Khanna
ZoomZoom (Flickr.com)

This Quarter

Has Asia's moment come?

Many commentators describe late 2008 and 2009 as the end of an era. Descriptions of the past 18 months often invoke the "return of Depression-era economics," the arrival of "black swans," or the myth of the "rational market." Although I agree we are witnessing profound changes to a certain model of global finance, I also think we'll come to see this period of time as a new beginning: the moment when the much-heralded Asian Century fully dawned.

Of course, Asia's arrival on the global stage has been widely discussed over several decades. This past year, however, has brought tantalizing signs that the day is truly at hand. The region has shown extraordinary resilience in the face of the worldwide slowdown. After a couple of tough quarters, China is barreling ahead again at better than 7 percent growth. India's growth has topped 6 percent. Even in Japan, where a new political party swept into power in a historic election, sentiment seems at last to be improving. Indeed, Asian economies now appear poised to lead a global recovery. When I meet with government and business leaders around the world, I find that discussions about Asian markets have a feeling of energy that's unusual in these challenging times. As I visit Asia's business hubs, what I sense above all is confi-dence—that living standards will resume their upward climb, stock and property markets will recover, and the region will bounce back stronger than ever.

Growth itself is hardly a new phenomenon in Asia. As *Time* journalist Michael Schuman so vividly shows in his new book, *The Miracle*, the rise of Asia's economies has been a four-decade marvel enabling hundreds of millions who might otherwise have been "stuck knee-deep in muddy rice paddies" to rise from poverty and aspire to levels of education and prosperity their grandparents never could have imagined. Yet as Morgan Stanley Asia chairman Stephen Roach points out in an interview in this issue, the Asian miracle has thus far depended heavily on government-led investment and policies designed to create low-cost platforms for exports to the West.

The current recession threatens this Asian model in a way the two previous global downturns didn't. Throughout the Asian financial crisis of the late 1990s and the US technology crash of 2001, the US consumer's appetite for products made in Asia kept growing, stoked by low interest rates and steady gains in home values. But that spending binge has finally run its course. The prospect of an extended slump in US private consumption has forced Asian economies to contemplate new ways of expanding trade among themselves and to stimulate consumption in their home markets.

In the near term, I expect Asia to push ahead with efforts to bolster intraregional commerce. The Asian Development Bank (ADB) recently reported that trade within the region rose to 54 percent of its total trade in 2007, up from 34 percent in 1980. The number of intra-regional free-trade agreements has increased to 54—up from just 3 in 2000—and the ADB says another 78 have been proposed or are under negotiation.

That's a welcome trend. But to sustain and extend the benefits of increased trade within the region, these economies must also encourage spending by their own consumers, so the time has come for Asia's leaders to fundamentally reexamine its current economic policies and institutions. Consider the case of China: although it's Asia's fastest-growing economy, the country still has the lowest consumption-to-GDP ratio—just 36 percent—ever seen in a major market economy. In "A consumer paradigm for China," an analysis of China's economic policies, the McKinsey Global Institute finds that the country could lift this ratio to more than 50 percent. But attaining that goal would require a concerted policy effort across a number of fronts for more than 15 years.

Even at current consumption rates, Asian markets offer compelling opportunities. As Yuval Atsmon and Vinay Dixit explain in "Understanding China's wealthy," China already has a large and rapidly growing pool of affluent consumers with a keen appetite for foreign brands. But for most large global consumer companies, the key to long-term success in Asia lies not in upscale niche markets but in selling at high volumes and dramatically lower price points than they find back in their home markets. In "Think regionally, act locally: Four steps to reaching the Asian consumer," Todd Guild contends that to compete successfully in Asia's fast-growing mass markets, these companies must rethink the most fundamental elements of the business models they use there. Global businesses can't hope to succeed in the new Asia by peddling products developed for consumers elsewhere. Indeed, we find that success in reaching Asian consumers demands an extraordinary product focus and marketing strategies tailored not only to individual countries but also, increasingly, to specific segments in particular urban clusters.

My own years of living and working in Asia have convinced me that establishing a leadership position there is a prize well worth the effort. For many companies, success in this region will provide the key to continued competitiveness in the new global economic order fast emerging from the events of a turbulent year.

Dominic Barton
Managing director,
McKinsey & Company

午后红茶

Afternoon Tea

Taking afternoon tea is a unique custom which is said to have started in the early 19th century.

HOLIDAY Courtesy of Paramount Pictures
n Hepburn Ferrer and Luca Dotti

有你, 有我, 更味乐!

奶茶　原味红茶　柠檬红茶　冰晶柠檬

Soctech (Flickr.com)

Stefano Amantini,
Atlantide Phototravel/Corbis

Lanchonqzi (Flickr.com)

Think regionally, act locally: Four steps to reaching the Asian consumer

The most successful global consumer enterprises are radically reshaping their organizations and business models to suit the region's rapidly evolving high-growth markets.

Todd Guild

Asia's emerging economies are leading the world out of recession, and the region's consumers are taking the baton from their over-extended counterparts in developed countries. Are the largest global consumer enterprises ready for this momentous shift?

McKinsey's experience suggests that even the most sophisticated multinationals must change significantly to realize Asia's growth potential. The region is as diverse as it is vast. Its markets come in a bewildering assortment of sizes and development stages, and its customers hail from a multitude of ethnic and cultural backgrounds. Their tastes and preferences evolve constantly. The speed and scale of change in Asian consumer markets can surprise even experienced executives. To meet the challenge, global companies will have to organize themselves regionally to coordinate strategy and use resources in the most efficient way while at the same time targeting the tastes of consumers on a very local level.

In Asia's high-growth markets, these companies face intense competition from low-cost local players; customers with modest incomes, disparate preferences, and minimal brand loyalties; and fragmented distribution channels. Some of the problems will recede as the region's economies mature. For now, though, the savviest players are trading their old management practices—including largely independent

Todd Guild is a director in McKinsey's Tokyo office.

country operations and centralized administrative structures—for leaner, faster, more flexible, and regionally collaborative ones. They are strengthening their in-country operations while creating small, fast, and entrepreneurial regional leadership teams, which at their most successful adeptly allocate resources across markets, leverage scarce executive talent, drive innovations from one market to another, and relentlessly cut costs.

Four general principles sum up the changes needed to reach Asia's new consumers through a strategy that's both regional and local. Global companies must revamp their corporate structures so that operations in Asia enjoy a high status commensurate with its long-term profit potential and have the autonomy needed for significant results. They have to focus on growth opportunities in urban clusters. Their products and prices must be tailored to local preferences. Finally, they must learn how to market, sell, and distribute products through a variety of channels and retail formats.

For global consumer companies, building this kind of regional–local structure can be an enormous challenge—but it can't be ignored. Instead of treating Asia as a sideshow, they must act on the assumption that success in Asian markets is necessary for survival.

Go where the growth is
Asia won't replace the United States as the lead engine of global growth—at least not for five to ten years. At the end of 2008, the GDP of the whole of Asia was just under $14 trillion, roughly the same as the GDP of the United States alone. Private consumption accounted for only about half of Asia's GDP, compared with 72 percent in the United States. Asia's three billion people spent less than $7 trillion; America's 300 million, upward of $10 trillion.[1] If Asia fails to stoke internal consumption, the region may grow more slowly over the next decade than it did in the last (see "A consumer paradigm for China," also in this issue). Yet some observers think private consumption in the region's emerging economies could grow enough, as early as this year, to offset falling consumption in the United States and the European Union. Even under dour assumptions about the prospects for Asian economies, the region is likely to contribute more than half of all growth in global consumption by 2020.

Such macroeconomic perspectives understate Asia's significance for individual companies. In dozens of product categories, the Asian consumer is already global king. China is the world's biggest market

[1] Global Insight. Unless otherwise noted, Asia as used in this article comprises the following economies: Australia, Bangladesh, Bhutan, Brunei, Cambodia, China, Hong Kong, India, Indonesia, Japan, Laos, Malaysia, Maldives, Mongolia, Nepal, New Zealand, the Pacific Islands, Pakistan, the Philippines, Singapore, South Korea, Sri Lanka, Taiwan, Thailand, and Vietnam.

for many household products, including TVs, refrigerators, and air conditioners. This year, for the first time ever, China will probably top the United States and Japan as the world's largest automobile market by number of vehicles sold. China's rank may slip back again as sales in those two advanced economies recover. Even so, with China's car ownership at fewer than 14 vehicles per thousand citizens, compared with more than 400 per thousand in the United States, the long-term trend is clear. For manufacturers such as GM and Volkswagen,

Japan's frustrations in China

Brian Salsberg

Japanese companies were among the earliest to enter China when it opened its doors to foreigners, three decades ago. The leading Japanese brewer Suntory, for example, was the first foreign company to form a joint venture in China's beer market. Lawson, Japan's second-largest convenience store chain, was the first overseas retailer to get a franchise in Shanghai. But discouraging experiences in the early years created a sense of skepticism about the prospects for long-term success.

Today, Japan's consumer companies lag far behind their global rivals in China, despite that early market entry, geographic proximity, and the Chinese consumer's high regard for the quality of Japanese brands. A McKinsey analysis of 12 consumer-facing industries found that, except for a few standouts in areas such as automotive and skincare, Japan's leading consumer companies struggle in China. Some have abandoned hope of building success-ful businesses there and are focusing on other areas, such as Southeast Asia. Sectors where Japanese companies have had particular difficulty include packaged foods, personal care, household care, PCs, and mobile handsets.

A McKinsey survey of senior executives at more than 30 leading Japanese companies (primarily in the consumer sector) found that the respondents generally saw China as an essential market. Yet many acknowl-edged that their companies had experienced only limited success there and expressed feelings of frustration, even futility, about the possibilities for improvement. A surprising

number thought it was too late to establish a significant presence.

Almost all the respondents expected less than 10 percent of their companies' revenues to come from China over the next three to five years; more than half said less than 5 per-cent. More than 70 percent of the respondents thought that now is the right time for further investments in China; 21 percent said that it's already too late or that they felt unsure whether investments make sense now. Sixty percent reported that Chinese nationals accounted for less than a tenth of the executives their companies employ in China. Only 25 percent said that they have programs to let Chinese executives spend time in Japan. Respondents at just two companies characterized their Chinese operations as 'highly independent' from headquarters.

Many respondents expressed frustration with China's weak legal and regulatory systems, but they acknowledged the problems their com-panies have in managing government relat-ions, attracting capable Chinese employees, and tailoring products to the needs and budgets of local consumers. Those difficulties are all the more striking given China's strategic importance to companies based in Japan, whose home market is mature and shrinking. For many Japanese consumer companies, success in China could prove the key to global competitiveness—or even survival.

Brian Salsberg is a principal in McKinsey's Tokyo office.

which made big bets in China early, booming sales there help offset home market losses. Later arrivals like Ford and the big Japanese carmakers (see sidebar "Japan's frustrations in China") are scrambling to catch up.

No company illustrates Asia's potential better than Yum! Brands, the proprietor of KFC and Pizza Hut. KFC opened its first restaurant on China's mainland in 1987, now operates 2,497 in the country (compared with 5,253 in the United States), and counts on it for nearly 30 percent of global revenue. Yum!'s total sales there, which soared 31 percent last year, helped the company shrug off the US recession. CEO David Novak, who tells investors that Yum!'s business in China is merely "in the first inning of a nine-inning ball game," vows the company will eventually have more than 20,000 restaurants in the country. He says KFC in China "can be every bit as big as McDonald's in the US."

But for many global companies with operations in China, a new phase is about to begin. The past decade was a time of market entry and gradual increase in scale. In the coming decade, overseas players will push for market leadership. India's consumer market lags behind China's by five to ten years, but similar stories of booming growth are unfolding there. Already, India is the world's fastest-growing mobile-phone market, adding more than ten million new subscribers a month. Its top consumer companies, including Hindustan Unilever, Nestlé India, Godrej Consumer Products, and Colgate Palmolive, have posted cumulative annual growth rates of 14 to 19 percent over the past five years while sales at the country's leading retailer, Pantaloon Retail, soared by 68 percent. Throughout Asia, products and market segments are growing explosively, in sudden waves of 70 to 100 percent expansion that could run for years. Global businesses that can't ride those waves may drown in them.

Change the game

Asia's emerging markets are a hypercompetitive free-for-all. Local rivals offer products with incremental innovations in ever-shorter product cycles—typically, at prices global companies find hard to match. Consumers don't know established global brands and show little loyalty to the brands they do know. Marketing strategies are complicated by the uneven development of Asia's telecom networks. The predominance of small, family-owned retail outlets thwarts efforts to control the distribution and display of products. For global consumer giants, fidelity to methods that work back home can be futile.

Leverage innovation and talent through regional teams

One key to success is rethinking organizational models. Many global companies try to use an international division run from the global home office to supervise their operations in Asia. Companies with large operations there may well have a regional headquarters, but often it oversees an assortment of country-specific fiefdoms that don't collaborate and sometimes operate in their own languages, frustrating communication. For Asia, that's often the worst model, leaving C-level executives at headquarters two layers from the most important growth markets, oblivious to the speed of change and the scale of the opportunity.

So global consumer companies are experimenting with alternative management practices and organizational models to ensure that Asian operations get the capital, talent, and C-level attention they need to compete. Some companies organize Asian operations as independent business units, with their own capital budgets, partnerships, and P&Ls. Yum! Brands, for instance, has three divisions: the United States, China, and elsewhere. In 2008, after years of running retail operations in China and Japan separately, Wal-Mart Stores established an Asia office in Hong Kong to spread best practices across the region.

Often, successful Asian organizational models involve teams of senior executives with diverse cultural and market experiences, who work together to improve performance throughout the region. These regional teams set priorities, as well as mobilize expertise and resources to achieve scale advantages that can't be realized at the level of any single Asian market. They plan strategically; drive supply chain and cost-cutting initiatives; oversee recruitment, product development, and strategic alliances; and make crucial decisions about distribution channels, formats, and categories. Collaboration and a sense of entrepreneurial pace characterize these regional teams. Top executives and specialists hop around markets, encouraging product designers in China, for example, to learn from innovations in Japan or a supply chain leader in India or to investigate techniques that simplified operations and lowered costs in Malaysia. According to many executives, getting managers throughout the region to speak a common language is essential for spreading such best practices.

'In China, consumer technology and infrastructure are blending together to create a once-in-a-lifetime opportunity for companies who understand the market.'

–Ed Chan,
President and CEO,
Wal-Mart China

Watch a video interview with Ed Chan, in which he discusses the challenges and opportunities of the Chinese market, on mckinseyquarterly.com.

Think cities, not regions or countries

To be effective in Asia, consumer companies must think regionally but sell locally: they do better by focusing on urban clusters than by conceiving of an entire country as one market. In recent years, many multinationals have tried to understand Asian markets more precisely by dividing them into subnational megaregions or attempting to craft multi-tier urban strategies based on population size or household income. Because these approaches miss crucial variations in consumer preferences and behavior, resources are invested less than optimally. McKinsey's experience suggests that in Asia, urban clusters are the most appropriate strategic and marketing unit for consumer businesses. Often, we advise clients to forget the forest and see the trees.

In developed and emerging Asia alike, cities are by far the dominant nodes of mass consumption, and their importance will surely grow. In Japan, more than half of all consumers live in Tokyo or Osaka. A fifth of South Korea's live in Seoul. In China, the McKinsey Global Institute estimates, more than 350 million people will leave the countryside by 2025, creating more than 23 megacities with populations upward of 5 million.[2] In India, more than 700 million people will make the same journey by 2050, creating as many as 36 megacities.

The current crisis has not only reduced the discretionary spending of Japanese consumers but also accelerated fundamental shifts in their attitudes and behavior. Visit mckinseyquarterly.com to read 'Japan's luxury consumers move on.'

The scale of these migrations has no precedent. They will create huge opportunities for global consumer companies—but also huge headaches. After pouring into the cities of China and India, the migrants will assume new social identities. They will be open to new foods, fashions, forms of entertainment, and ways of living, but they will be fickle customers unfamiliar with established brands. Asked to identify the top contenders in apparel, Asia's new urbanites are as apt to name local upstarts as, say, Louis Vuitton or Gucci.

As they prosper, their preferences will probably grow more diverse. In 2005, when McKinsey initiated extensive surveys of Chinese consumers, we found that the size and GDP of the cities where they lived predicted their spending habits reliably. People who lived in Beijing, Shanghai, and other first-tier cities, for example, tended to buy similar products. Over the next three years, as the number of China's middle- and high-income households tripled, geography became more important. By 2008, city of residence predicted 9 out of 12 of these attitudes. (For more, see sidebar "Understanding China's wealthy.")

Thus, in recent years, the market for premium refrigerators has grown by 20 percent in Shanghai but by only 8 percent in neighboring Nanjing. Consumers in Guangzhou are much more likely to buy cameras with sophisticated LCD screens than those in Shenzhen, another

---

[2] For the full McKinsey Global Institute report, see *Preparing for China's urban billion*, available free of charge online at mckinsey.com/mgi.

first-tier city only 100 kilometers away, who demand portable, thin models. Global companies must think carefully about where and how to play in Asia's urban markets.

Customize locally, don't tweak

Long gone are the days when global companies could charge Asians a premium to buy products designed for consumers in developed markets. It's not enough even to tweak existing product lines for Asian sensibilities. Success now requires the ability not only to understand regional and local tastes and preferences but also to design products and services in Asia.

South Korea's LG Electronics struggled when it came to India in the 1990s until a change in foreign-investment rules enabled the company to invest in local design and manufacturing facilities.[3] Noting, for example, that many Indians use their TVs to listen to music, LG introduced new models with better speakers and, to keep prices competitive, less costly displays. The company marketed many other original products, including appliances with programming menus in local languages, refrigerators with brighter colors and smaller freezers, large washing machines for India's big families, and microwaves with one-touch "Indian menu" functions. Those innovations were possible because LG invested heavily in local R&D and staffed its operations with thousands of top-notch Indian designers and engineers. LG's product innovation center in Bangalore is the company's largest outside South Korea. The company is India's market leader in TVs, refrigerators, air conditioners, and washing machines.

Local design is all the more important in Asia because customers in many of its markets expect a very wide variety of offerings and short innovation cycles. Yum! Brands' Pizza Hut restaurants in China sell as much Chinese food as pizza, and in 2004 the company launched a new chain, East Dawning, that serves only Chinese food. KFC tailors menus to local palates and launches new items every month. Tingyi, the Taiwanese company that is the mainland's leading instant-noodle vendor, used local designers to reshape a whole product category, creating separate premium and low-cost brands.

In Asia, price is a crucial part of customization. For all but a few categories, volume—not a high profit margin—is the key to sustainable success. Products in categories such as apparel, automotive, and consumer electronics are sinking to price points that were unthinkable only a few years ago. What's more, sophisticated consumer companies like P&G and Hindustan Lever have repeatedly found that compelling entry-level products and brands are essential for attracting

[3] See Pramath Raj Sinha, "Premium marketing to the masses: An interview with LG Electronics India's managing director," mckinseyquarterly.com, September 2005.

(continued on page 34)

Understanding China's wealthy

Yuval Atsmon and
Vinay Dixit

For many companies around the world, wealthy consumers in China represent a rare opportunity in an otherwise dismal picture. Despite the global downturn, their ranks continue to grow. By 2015, the country will hold the world's fourth-largest concentration of wealthy people.

The number of China's wealthy households, which hit 1.6 million in 2008, will climb to more than 4.4 million by 2015, trailing only those in the United States, Japan, and the United Kingdom in sheer size (with definitions of wealth adjusted for purchasing-power parity). Despite the current economic slowdown, the number of wealthy households in China will probably expand at an annual rate of about 16 percent for the next five to seven years.

Our research, which included face-to-face interviews in 16 cities with 1,750 wealthy Chinese consumers, shows that one of their clearest distinguishing features is their youth: some 80 percent are under 45, compared with 30 percent in the United States and 19 percent in Japan. Because they are newer to the

Yuval Atsmon is an associate principal in McKinsey's Shanghai office, where **Vinay Dixit** leads McKinsey's Insights China.

consumer market and to wealth, they are less knowledgeable about luxury brands. They also value the functional benefits of products (quality, materials, design, or craftsmanship, for instance) more than their counterparts elsewhere do.

What's more, wealthy Chinese are very different from the rest of the country. The gap in attitudes and behavior is particularly stark when we compare them with the mainstream: for example, 52 percent said that they trusted foreign brands, compared with only 11 percent of mainstream consumers. The wealthy also are more willing to try new technology, more amenable to borrowing, and more likely to have difficulty maintaining a satisfactory work–life balance.

Like Chinese consumers in general, the wealthy watch a lot of television, but they spend more time surfing the Internet than do members of other income groups. Wealthy people in China also spend more time outside their homes, engaging in sports, visiting health spas, and drinking and dining out. Indeed, the wealthy

Exhibit: **Seven segments**

A needs-based analysis uncovered seven distinct segments among China's wealthy consumers.

Luxuriant

Located mainly in tier-1 cities; higher proportion of women

Care about health, environment, and quality of family life

Passionate about luxury goods, but quality matters more than brand

Flashy

Greater numbers in tier-1 cities

Care less about health, environment; go out of their way to find cheapest price

Big luxury-goods spenders: brand is important yet prepared to buy look-alike products

Urbane

Greater numbers in tier-1 cities; higher proportion of males

Care about health, environment, and quality of family life

Sophisticated but low key; care more about product quality than brand—against look-alike products

Share of total wealth

Luxuriant = 22%	Flashy = 22%	Urbane = 14%
$85,000	$78,000	$73,000

Average household income[1]

[1] $1 = 7 renminbi in 2008.

Source: 2008 McKinsey survey of wealthy Chinese consumers

© Gilles Sabrié

spend 17 percent of their household income dining out (compared with 7 percent for mainstream consumers) and 10 percent on leisure and entertainment (compared with 3 percent for the mainstream).

China's wealthy consumers differ not only from their global peers and from other Chinese but also from one another. Yet easily obtained demographic information—age, gender, and income, for instance—offers little help in separating China's wealthy into segments with differing attitudes toward, say, fashion, borrowing, or obvious displays of wealth. More meaningful differences emerged when we considered what respondents said about their needs—the need to feel unique, for example, or to feel financially secure. This needs-based analysis uncovered seven distinct segments among China's wealthy consumers (exhibit).

Consumers in the 'luxuriant' segment, for example, are among the country's wealthiest people, passionate about the finest products and services. They never settle for less than the best and gravitate toward high-end, high-fashion brands, such as Hermès and Chanel. These consumers are a brand's best friend, buying frequently and talking with friends about their purchases.

Compare this segment with the 'demanding' one: self-made men and women who may have more money than they need and are satisfied with their success, although they still work hard. They don't have a taste for luxury goods, especially fashion; rarely buy the very best; often are content with look-alikes; and make an effort to compare prices before buying, even at prices they can easily afford.

Only by understanding how China's wealthy households differ from those in other markets, from other Chinese consumers, and from one another can companies win the trust and loyalty of this attractive group and help shape its evolving tastes and buying behavior.

Demanding	**Enthusiast**	**Down to earth**	**Climber**
Wealthier than most yet are hardest working; dislike borrowing	Greater numbers in tier-2 cities	Greater numbers in tier-2 cities; younger and newer to wealth	Greater numbers in tier-2 and -3 cities
May splurge on products to stand out from the crowd	Enthusiastic about luxury goods; want to buy more than they can afford, want to stand out from the crowd	Value family life over social life	Status conscious; keen to socialize with the influential
Less willing to pay for the best; hard to please	Prepared to buy look-alike products; favor Chinese brands	Care little about higher-end products or foreign brands	Appreciate luxury goods but not as a necessity; go out of their way to find cheapest price

Demanding = 13%	Enthusiast = 11%	Down to earth = 10%	Climber = 8%
$84,000	$69,000	$70,000	$71,000

The full version of this article is available on mckinseyquarterly.com.

consumers to higher-priced ones, often by "de-engineering" premium products to focus on the features and attributes that Asian customers value most. P&G, for example, cut the price of Crest toothpaste more than 50 percent in China by reducing the cost of packaging, which, they learned, is less important to consumers than being able to choose from a variety of flavors.

Financing can play a role too. Levi Strauss recently announced that it would let customers in India pay in three monthly installments for jeans costing more than $33. A pilot version of the program, in Bangalore, showed the company that consumers who took advantage of this option spent an average of 50 percent more. Introducing it enabled Levi Strauss to preserve the status of its jeans as an upmarket, aspirational product, while bringing them within reach of millions of less affluent young consumers.

Related articles on mckinseyquarterly.com

Making China your second home market:
An interview with the CEO of Danfoss

Bringing best practice to China

The Chinese consumer: To spend or to save?

In pushing prices lower, supply chain management matters no less than financing and design. Asia's savviest consumer businesses have embraced the techniques pioneered by fast-fashion retailers and Japanese automakers in picking up the pace and lowering the costs of the entire supply chain. LG, for instance, has shortened order-fulfillment cycles in Asia from months to just weeks. Retailers and consumer product companies are learning that fast supply chains for some categories assure fresher products and a quicker response to trends in everything from fashion to consumer electronics.

Learn to market and sell across a variety of channels

Penetration rates for traditional and online media are lower in developing Asia than in developed markets, so efforts to influence purchase decisions are more complex. Consumer companies must be adept at shaping the consumers' view of brands across a number of channels and through a variety of media—not only TV, radio, print, and the Internet, but also events, outdoor ads, mobile messaging, in-store promotions, and educational campaigns. Managing this shift to multichannel retailing and sales calls for new approaches to marketing and brand building.

Modern retail chains account for only about a third of all consumer goods sales in China and for less than a fifth in India; small, family-run shops are much more important. In all formats, consumer product companies must somehow influence access to shelf space and display, since point-of-sale factors have an ever greater impact on purchase decisions. For now, key-account management is less important in Asia than it is in developed markets. Many global companies get things wrong because they attempt to rely on the sales teams of third-party distributors and the key-account-management routines that worked at home or in the past.

Adapting quickly to capture growth from direct-to-consumer channels will also probably become more important in Asia, as it already is elsewhere. In some urban clusters, for categories such as consumer electronics and apparel, online sales growth is beginning to overtake traditional channels. In Japan, sales in direct channels have exceeded those in department stores so far this year. Sales at TaoBao, China's largest online retailer, have soared to more than $14 billion annually since it was launched, in 2003. Lancôme reports that its partnership with Baidu, China's largest search engine, helped lift online sales in China by 30 percent. And AmWay has become one of China's largest consumer packaged-goods companies by selling its products door-to-door through a network of 300,000 sales representatives.

• • •

As Asia's economies evolve and mature, today's frenetic, hypercompetitive, fragmented marketplace will inevitably give way to a more settled one, with fewer players enjoying larger market shares and better margins. The penetration of modern retail formats will increase. But the journey will be long and filled with twists and turns.

The author wishes to acknowledge the contributions of Yuval Atsmon, Tiffany Lee, Jennifer Li, Evelyn Lu, Max Magni, Ireena Vittal, and Ming Zhang to this article.

Copyright © 2009 McKinsey & Company. All rights reserved.

We welcome your comments on this article. Please send them to quarterly_comments@ mckinsey.com.

As the winners learn to make decisions quickly to meet the demand for speed, scale, localization, and low costs, they will test and adopt new and more entrepreneurial management practices. These companies will probably share four characteristics. Their fast, adaptive business models will leverage scale and innovation throughout Asia, and regional organizational structures and operating practices will reflect this shift. But resources will be focused locally, on the development of category, format, and brand strategies targeting the explosive growth opportunities of sharply defined urban clusters, not countries. Products tailored and priced to meet cluster-level tastes and needs will be supported by faster, lower-cost supply chains. Finally, brand marketing skills will be used to market and sell across a variety of channels. For global consumer businesses, the struggle for Asia has now been joined—cluster by cluster, city by city. ○

Philippe Lopez, AFP/
Getty Images

Jon Hicks/Corbis

A consumer paradigm for China

A more consumer-centric economy would allocate capital and resources more efficiently, generate more jobs, and spread the benefits of growth more equitably. It would also even grow more rapidly.

Janamitra Devan, Micah Rowland, and Jonathan Woetzel

The development paradigm that brought China two decades of rapid growth and lifted millions of people out of poverty is reaching the limits of its utility. Well before the US credit bubble imploded, China's leaders recognized that this old economic model, with its heavy reliance on exports and government-led investments, was straining at the seams.[1] The global recession that followed Lehman Brothers' collapse put the model's drawbacks into sharp relief. When exports plunged, factories closed, and millions of Chinese migrants lost their jobs, Beijing responded with a $600 billion stimulus package and a torrent of new lending by state-owned banks.

Janamitra Devan is an alumnus of the McKinsey Global Institute; **Micah Rowland** is a consultant in McKinsey's Seattle office, and **Jonathan Woetzel** is a director in the Shanghai office.

But those remedies, while highly successful in restoring short-term growth, risk aggravating structural distortions that made China's economy vulnerable to external-demand shocks in the first place. As the global crisis ebbs, China's leaders realize more clearly than ever that they must unleash consumer spending to achieve sustainable growth. Stoking Chinese consumption has vaulted to the top of national—indeed global—policy agendas. But how, and how much, can it be raised?

[1] In March 2007, Premier Wen Jiabao used the occasion of his annual nationally televised press conference after the National People's Congress to issue a rare public warning that China's economy had become "unbalanced, uncoordinated, unstable, and unsustainable." See Joseph Kahn, "Despite buildup, China insists its goals are domestic," *New York Times*, March 17, 2007.

To answer that question, the McKinsey Global Institute (MGI) considered three scenarios for Chinese consumption rates over the next 15 years: a base case (no new action to raise consumption), a policy case (full implementation of proconsumption measures already announced), and a stretch case (a push beyond the current agenda to implement broad changes in the economy's structure).

MGI estimates that in the base case, China's consumption will rise to 39 percent of GDP, a gain of just three percentage points above the current level, leaving the country heavily dependent on exports and government-led spending for continued growth. In the policy scenario, consumption could account for as much as 45 percent of GDP, still well below levels in other major economies. If China's leaders committed themselves to the more aggressive program of comprehensive reform envisioned in the stretch scenario, however, they could raise private consumption above 50 percent of GDP by 2025 (Exhibit 1). Clearing that threshold would bring the consumption rate in line with those in the developed nations of Europe and Asia, vaulting China's economy into a new phase. McKinsey estimates that comprehensive reform would also enrich the global economy with $1.9 trillion a year in net new consumption, boosting China's share of the worldwide total to 13 percent—four percentage points higher than its share without further effort.

Exhibit 1: **Tools for raising consumption**

Aggressive moves will be needed to raise China's rate of consumption.

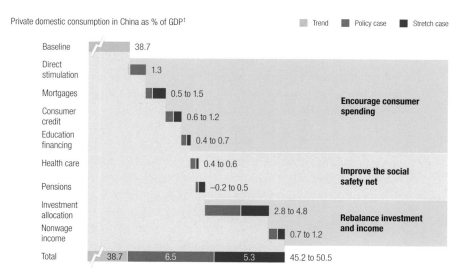

Private domestic consumption in China as % of GDP[1]

| | Trend | Policy case | Stretch case |

Baseline	38.7	
Direct stimulation	1.3	Encourage consumer spending
Mortgages	0.5 to 1.5	
Consumer credit	0.6 to 1.2	
Education financing	0.4 to 0.7	
Health care	0.4 to 0.6	Improve the social safety net
Pensions	−0.2 to 0.5	
Investment allocation	2.8 to 4.8	Rebalance investment and income
Nonwage income	0.7 to 1.2	
Total	38.7 6.5 5.3 45.2 to 50.5	

[1] In real 2000 dollars.

Source: Global Insight; McKinsey Global Institute analysis

Reaching the stretch target wouldn't be easy. China's leaders will have to wage a sustained policy struggle on many fronts, combining relatively straightforward measures to encourage private spending with fundamental reform of the nation's health and pension systems and sweeping changes in the economy's basic structure. Over the next 15 years, China can realistically hope to increase private consumption's share of total GDP significantly—but only if policy makers depart from the current development paradigm and embrace new policies, structures, and institutions better suited to the country's status as a large, maturing market economy. That transformation, though daunting, would have a worthy prize: a more stable and fair economy that uses resources more efficiently, creates more jobs, insulates its citizens from foreign-trade shocks, and contributes more substantially to global growth.

China's constrained consumers

In seeking to bolster private consumption, China's policy makers face a unique challenge. Although there is no generally accepted standard for "healthy" private consumption in developing economies, in China it is anemic by almost any measure. Private consumption there totaled $890 billion in 2007, making the country the world's fifth-largest consumer market, behind the United States, Japan, the United Kingdom, and Germany (which China recently surpassed as the world's third-largest economy). But relative to China's population and level of economic development, its consumers punch far below their weight. The country's consumption-to-GDP ratio—36 percent—is only half that of the United States and about two-thirds of what it is in Europe and Japan. Indeed, China has the lowest consumption-to-GDP ratio of any major world economy except Saudi Arabia, where oil exports contribute the bulk of economic output (Exhibit 2).

In fact, China's consumption-to-GDP ratio has dropped by nearly 15 percentage points since 1990 and continues to deteriorate in the

Exhibit 2: **Frugal China**

China's rate of consumption relative to GDP is low compared with those of other nations.

Private domestic consumption as % of GDP,[1] 2008

United States	71	India	57
United Kingdom	67	Japan	55
Brazil	65	Germany	54
Russia	62	**China**	**37**

[1] In real 2000 dollars.

Source: Global Insight; McKinsey Global Institute analysis

aftermath of the financial crisis. While falling consumption rates are common in developing economies, the speed and magnitude of this decline have no precedent in modern history. In the United States, private consumption remained above 50 percent of GDP even during the full-scale industrialization drive of World War II. In Japan and South Korea, consumption remained above 50 percent during periods of rapid industrial development.

The sources of China's low consumption rate are both behavioral and structural (see sidebar "China's consumption challenge: A round-table"). The country's households have an extraordinarily high ability to save: the average Chinese family squirrels away an astonishing 25 percent of its discretionary income, about six times the savings rate for US households and three times the rate for Japan's. Indeed, China's savings rate is 15 percentage points above the GDP-weighted average for Asia as a region.

Frugality's impact is compounded—and in many ways produced—by structural features that restrict consumption's share of the national income. For one thing, Chinese households command only some 56 percent of it (Exhibit 3), compared with more than 60 percent in Europe and more than 70 percent in the United States. No effort to raise Chinese consumption rates significantly can hope to succeed without addressing the structural factors that both channel income

Exhibit 3: **Household finances**

Households account for a relatively low and falling share of total income in China.

Household income as % of GDP[1]

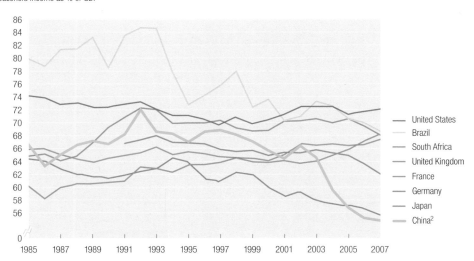

[1] In real 2000 dollars.
[2] Data prior to 2005 might be near 55% as well; income for small and midsize enterprises was systematically undercounted (leading to overstatement of household income share), although no revisions of these numbers have been made in official data.

Source: Global Insight; McKinsey Global Institute analysis

away from consumers and discourage them from spending even their modest share.

Mending the social safety net

Perhaps the most common explanation for the Chinese consumer's reluctance to spend more freely is the frayed social safety net. Many argue that the country's consumers oversave and underspend because they lack adequate health insurance and can't count on government- or employer-sponsored programs to provide for them in retirement (see sidebar "Looking ahead to the 'next Asia': An interview with the chairman of Morgan Stanley Asia"). The relationship between social-welfare programs and private consumption is complex, but the moral imperative to extend health and retirement protections to the millions of Chinese who lack them is clear. Over the long run, mending the social safety net would ease anxieties about the future and bolster consumer confidence.

But MGI believes that better health and pension guarantees wouldn't raise private consumption significantly before 2025. In assessing their impact on consumer spending, the key question to consider is who pays for them. If enhanced health and retirement benefits were financed through increased or expanded payroll taxes—a virtual certainty—households would feel less pressure to save, but after withholding they would have less money to spend. Thus the primary impact of expanding health and pension programs would be distributive, shifting to middle- and upper-income households the cost of benefits for poor ones. Moreover, any effort to broaden health insurance coverage would probably require a substantial increase in public outlays for medical care and thus raise the government's share of total consumption.

MGI's effort to model the reciprocal effects of such changes suggests that, in the aggregate, even a fully fledged program to expand China's health and retirement benefits wouldn't raise private consumption's share of GDP significantly. We estimate that, at best, such improvements would boost it by only a percentage point above the 2025 base-case projection.

Putting products within reach

Measures to make goods and services better and more easily available could encourage consumption much more than would fixing the social safety net. China's consumer infrastructure is incomplete. Too few products are tailored to the needs of those who would use them. Prices remain high compared with income levels: a Chinese worker toils more than seven hours to buy the same amount of goods and services a US worker earns through only one hour of work. In rural China—home to more than half of the country's 1.3 billion

(continued on page 44)

China's consumption challenge: A roundtable

The panelists

Bai Chong'en is a professor and chair of the Department of Economics at Tsinghua University.

Li Xiaoxi is the director of Beijing Normal University's Institute of Economic and Resource Management.

Cao Yuanzheng is the chief economist of Bank of China International.

Wang Xiaolu is the deputy director of the China Reform Foundation's National Economic Research Institute.

Bolstered by a $586 billion government stimulus program and a surge in lending by state-owned banks, China may be the first major economy to bounce back from the global recession. But the composition of growth remains unbalanced. The consumption ratio—spending by households as a percentage of GDP—is roughly half the US level and significantly below levels in Europe and Japan. China's ratio of private spending to GDP has actually fallen over the past decade. McKinsey director Jonathan Woetzel spoke with four distinguished Chinese economists and members of the McKinsey China Council of Business Economists about what's hampering Chinese consumption, as well as the prospects for spurring its growth. What follows is an excerpt from their conversation.

Jonathan Woetzel: *Private consumption accounts for roughly a third of China's GDP. Why is it so low?*

Wang Xiaolu: One reason is that China doesn't have a universal social-security system. Only about one-third of the urban population is covered by the social-security system, and few rural residents have social security at all. Also, over the past few years, the cost for education, medication, and housing has increased quite rapidly—much more rapidly than GDP growth and income growth.

Cao Yuanzheng: China's historical level for consumption, in terms of GDP, is over 50 percent. If we set this as a standard, we can see there is a gap of at least 15 percent.

Bai Chong'en: To fix this, it's very important to increase household incomes. Without income, no matter what happens households just don't have the means to consume.

Jonathan Woetzel: *What's the relationship between the social safety net and consumption?*

Bai Chong'en: When we increase spending on social security, private consumption doesn't necessarily increase. The answer depends on how social security is financed. Rural health insurance, for example, is subsidized by the government so there is no crowding out. Since rural residents didn't need to spend a lot to purchase insurance, consumption increased. But urban social security is mainly financed by payroll tax, and the tax rate is too high. We have five different insurances. If you add them together, the tax on labor income is around 40 percent—which is a lot. That kind of tax crowds out private consumption.

Jonathan Woetzel: *What are some short-term policies that could help?*

Bai Chong'en: We need to create more nonagricultural jobs. Employment growth in the industrial sector lags far behind GDP growth, and the 40 percent payroll tax on labor income is suppressing employment.

Li Xiaoxi: The global financial crisis has made our unemployment situation even worse, with factory closures and bankruptcy in the southeast coastal area. Many migrant workers who used to work there had to return home to the midwest. Helping them find new jobs is critical for boosting domestic consumption.

Jonathan Woetzel: *Can the Chinese government afford to increase consumption?*

Bai Chong'en: One source could be the profit of state-owned enterprises, especially those with monopoly power. The largest share of savings increase has been in the corporate sector. These savings were not controlled; they were invested in low-efficiency projects. So if the government forces these firms to pay higher dividends, it's actually one stone that kills two birds. You use that money to finance the social-security system so you have room to reduce payroll tax, and by stripping the money away from state-owned enterprises, their ability to invest is mitigated.

Jonathan Woetzel: *Is this a good time for China to be increasing consumption?*

Cao Yuanzheng: We have to because there's no way out. I think everyone now understands that.

Bai Chong'en: Normally, when per capita income goes beyond $3,000, consumption picks up rapidly. China is moving toward that threshold. However, this conventional wisdom may not give us much cause for optimism, because usually the consumption increase comes from housing and automobiles, and on both of these fronts we cannot follow the Western model—especially the US model. Recently, automobile sales have been increasing very rapidly, to everybody's surprise, but I don't think that's a very good sign. We just don't have enough oil available to let every Chinese household have a car and drive on gasoline.

Jonathan Woetzel: *What would increased consumption in China mean for the rest of the world?*

Li Xiaoxi: A dramatic jump in Chinese consumption is not necessarily a good thing, as the global economy is so interdependent. If China consumes all the goods, there may be nothing left for export. And if China doesn't export much, it won't have much cash to buy T-bonds from the US. It's difficult to have your cake and eat it too.

Bai Chong'en: Driving consumption for all these consumers—from China, India, and other countries—given our resource constraints, given our environmental constraints: that's the biggest challenge in the world.

This roundtable is adapted from a video interview, available on mckinseyquarterly.com.

consumers—organized retail establishments mediate only 18 percent of consumption, compared with 50 percent in urban areas.

Even when high-quality products are readily available, China's consumers hesitate to buy them on credit. At 3 percent of GDP, outstanding consumer debt in China falls well below that of other large developing countries, such as Brazil, at 12 percent, or Russia, at 7 percent (see sidebar "China's fast-evolving consumer finance market"). What's more, the privatization of China's housing stock created a

Looking ahead to the 'next Asia':
An interview with the chairman of Morgan Stanley Asia

Clay Chandler

Stephen Roach, chairman of Morgan Stanley Asia, is a longtime observer of the region and the global economy. In this interview excerpt, Roach reflects on the Asian consumer's increasingly important role in the world economy. The interview was conducted by Clay Chandler, an editor with McKinsey Publishing, in August 2009 at Morgan Stanley Asia's headquarters, in Hong Kong.

The *Quarterly*: *Your new book is called* The Next Asia.[1] *What will be different about the next Asia, and what's driving those changes?*

Stephen Roach: The Asia of the past 30 years has done an extraordinary job—especially China but, increasingly, the rest of the region as well—in lifting standards of living faster than anything we've seen in the modern annals of economic development. But the drivers have been primarily export led, accompanied by a lot of investment in the export-production and -delivery platform that has been required for that export machine. This model is close to having outlived its usefulness. Number one, it's unbalanced. Asia needs more internal private consumption than it has right now. And number two, if all there is to Asia is an export machine, that ultimately runs a real risk of trade frictions with the rest of the world. The next Asia will be more consumer led. It will have a dynamic that also places greater emphasis on the quality of the growth experience, especially in terms of environmental protection and pollution control.

Clay Chandler is an editor with McKinsey Publishing.

The *Quarterly*: *What are the implications of those differences for CEOs of multinationals?*

Stephen Roach: Until now, multinationals primarily have viewed developing Asia, and China in particular, as an offshore-production platform—an efficiency solution for moving some of their high-cost operations offshore. I think the offshore-efficiency solution is still attractive. But what really could be powerful would be a growing opportunity to tap into the region's 3.5 billion consumers. This has been the dream, all along, of the Asian potential.

The *Quarterly*: *Why should Asia move to a consumer-led growth strategy? Why not stick with the investment- and export-led approach that's worked so well?*

Stephen Roach: Because the US-led external demand that has underpinned the export model is now in serious trouble. Even if Asia is the best and most efficient producer that anyone has ever seen, the external demand is not going to have the vigor it once did. So if Asia wants to keep growing, to keep developing, to keep raising the standard of living for its consumers, it's got to depend more on its own internal demand. Asia's development options have narrowed as never before.

The *Quarterly*: *Aren't we beginning to see some signs of a global recovery?*

powerful new imperative to save: only the most affluent urban families can obtain mortgages, which thus account for just 23 percent of the value of new homes in China, compared with 65 percent in the United States.

Similarly, concerns about financing the cost of a university education drive much of China's saving: an April 2009 survey of urban Chinese households commissioned by MGI found that this was the number-one reason for it, eclipsing concerns about medical expenses and retirement.

Stephen Roach is chairman of Morgan Stanley Asia. He has been with the company since 1982.

Stephen Roach: The next America will be the reverse image of the next Asia. Over the past decade, Asia was able to export because the American consumer went on the mother of all spending binges. What made that possible was that American consumers borrowed against an asset bubble.

But that bubble has now burst. So here's the US consumer, who's made this big bet and it's gone wrong. Now he has to pull back. He's getting older. He's got too much debt, not enough savings. All that excess spending has to give way to a rebuilding of savings. And export-led Asian economies need to respond to that new reality. If they don't, their growth is at risk.

The *Quarterly*: *In your book, you write that the consumer is the soul of the new Asia. How can we be sure?*

Stephen Roach: This will happen by necessity and not because of the spontaneous exuberance of over three billion consumers. There is an important missing piece in the equation. Asian governments need to build up the social safety net—social security, private-sector pensions, medical insurance, unemployment insurance.

A true safety net would give consumers and households throughout the region the confidence to draw down their excess savings. If Asian governments start to go down that road, then I think you will see a reduction of surplus savings and see those funds funneled into a more dynamic consumer culture.

The *Quarterly*: *How much can China hope to lift consumption as a percentage of GDP?*

Stephen Roach: I've learned in my years of following China not to underestimate the determination of the Chinese authorities to address a problem when they finally realize they've got a serious one. I think a realistic goal would be to aim for a 50 percent share of GDP for Chinese consumption within five years. A shift of 14 percentage points in the mix of GDP in five years. But I think it's achievable if China moves aggressively on social security, pensions, and nationwide medical care.

The *Quarterly*: *What are the obstacles?*

Stephen Roach: Mainly persuading an entire generation of Chinese workers and families— who have lost their 'iron rice bowl' through the reform of state-owned enterprises—that it's okay to begin to draw down excess savings. People say, 'Oh, the high savings rate is a cultural thing in Asia.' I don't buy that for a second. Excess savings were an outgrowth of necessity rather than cultural DNA. Alleviate income insecurity and those habits can change surprisingly quickly.

[1] *Stephen Roach on the Next Asia: Opportunities and Challenges for a New Globalization,* Hoboken, NJ: Wiley, 2009.

Watch the full video interview with Stephen Roach on mckinseyquarterly.com.

In China, local governments provide for primary and secondary education. But surveys suggest that nearly nine in ten Chinese households hope to send their children to colleges, where costs are high relative to incomes—on average, the cost of a university education is nearly half the disposable income of a typical Chinese family. China has two national student loan programs, but only 10 percent of its college students now participate in them.

MGI estimates that, in the aggregate, measures to facilitate consumer spending—through better and more easily available products and expanded access to consumer credit and to financing for a university education—could raise consumption's 2025 share of GDP by 2.8 to 4.7 percentage points.

Restructuring an investment-centric economy

Over time, a stronger social safety net and improved access to better goods and services will encourage China's households to save less and spend more. But the country can't hope to increase its consumption rate meaningfully unless it reverses a major current trend: households have a small and shrinking share of the national income. Any significant rise in household incomes will in turn require far-reaching policy changes that would transform some of the economy's most basic structures. The fundamental causes of depressed consumption rates are systemic—hardwired into a development model that values investment over household income—rather than unique consumer preferences rooted in culture.

China's current growth model tilts overwhelmingly in favor of large industrial companies, which typically are state owned or led, benefit from preferential financing from state-controlled banks, and enjoy considerable monopoly power. These features collectively place consumers at a disadvantage and limit employment growth. In any economy, large companies in heavy industry tend to be capital intensive, requiring fewer workers per unit of output than smaller firms in light industries or the service sector. In China, state ownership of heavy industry magnifies this tendency.

China's fast-evolving consumer finance market

Jan Bellens,
Stephan Bosshart,
and Dan Ewing

China's consumer finance industry lags far behind the economy as a whole. In 2007, consumer finance balances still came to less than 13 percent of GDP, below India and far below Singapore and South Korea. Should recent growth rates persist, consumer lending promises to exceed 8 trillion renminbi ($1.2 trillion) by 2014, up from today's 3.7 trillion renminbi.[1] But that calculation understates the market's latent potential. If consumer lending on the mainland rose to Taiwan's level, for instance, the shift could unleash as much as 10 trillion renminbi in net new consumption over the next five years—an enormous opportunity for banks and retailers.

China's people now have limited credit options. Mortgages account for 90 percent of lending to consumers, who have few choices in key product areas, such as auto loans, credit cards, and personal loans. But the market has grown rapidly in recent years. Credit card issuance is skyrocketing, from 3 million cards in 2003 to 128 million by the end of 2008. Indeed, card issuance could surpass 300 million by 2013. Similarly, unsecured personal loans and installment loans, long the domain of underground lenders, have grown at an annual rate of 33 percent since 2006, to 744 billion renminbi, as leading domestic banks and consumer finance specialists strengthened their risk-management capabilities.

For foreign and local lenders jockeying for position in China's fast-evolving consumer finance market, we see several keys to success.

1. Recognize the market's diversity.

China is a collection of local markets, each at a different stage of development, with distinct risk profiles and unique consumer preferences. These markets generally evolve through three stages of development: nascent (such as Sichuan), emerging (Jiangsu), and maturing (Shanghai). Lenders should take a portfolio view, focusing on the most promising markets, but with enough diversity to capture the next wave of growth.

2. Find a product portfolio that matches consumer preferences.

In a sense, consumer-lending products are fungible. Many consumers balance their savings and borrowing in the aggregate, not by individual products. Some countries (such as South Korea) have high levels of credit card usage; others rely more on cash and personal loans. In the present early stage, the ultimate product balance in China remains to be determined. Finding the right mix may prove crucial to success in China's fast-growing market.

3. Know the rules and their evolution.

New regulations issued by Chinese banking regulators in the spring of 2009 give local and foreign banks and consumer finance specialists greater access to the market, in the form of consumer finance companies. While initially restricted to offering installment loans to retail customers with previous track records in borrowing, such companies will probably enable attackers to participate in the unsecured consumer-lending sector more quickly and at greater scale. In addition, the further deregulation of credit cards has allowed overseas banks to issue renminbi-based ones. These banks should target clear segments and develop the ability to serve the broader market.

Would-be players in such a new market must tread carefully. To assure responsible lending and borrowing, the government must strengthen credit bureaus, improve financial education, support 'new to credit' products (for instance, low-limit or collateralized credit cards), and allow consumer finance balances to be securitized. Regulators and lenders must work together to improve risk management, especially the ability to identify and address organized fraud. The government must become better at spotting national and local credit bubbles. China can manage the risks and has ample room to expand consumer credit—safely.

[1] This assumes a 2008–14 compound annual growth rate (CAGR) of 14 percent for all consumer lending. Taiwan's ratio of consumer loans to GDP is 29 percent.

Jan Bellens is a principal in McKinsey's Shanghai office, where Stephan Bosshart is an associate principal; Dan Ewing is a consultant in the San Francisco office.

Such companies, which can count on ready access to capital from China's big banks and don't have to pay dividends on state-owned shares, have ample funds to plow back into capital investment. Large, state-led manufacturers tend to have monopoly power in their industries, making it easier to resist pressure from workers for higher wages.

The result is an economy dominated by giant, capital-intensive manufacturers with strong incentives to pile profits back into ever more plants and equipment rather than disburse them to households as dividends or wages. Labor-intensive producers— small and medium-sized enterprises—and the services sector get short shrift. Over the past two decades, the corporate share of China's national income has risen to 22 percent, up from 14 percent, even as the share of households has fallen to 56 percent, down from 72 percent. Media images of the country's factories teeming with workers belie the reality: the economy generates too few jobs given its size and rapid expansion. In recent years, employment growth has inched forward at a rate of 1 percent per year even as GDP advanced by double digits.

Related articles on mckinseyquarterly.com

Encouraging consumer spending in China

The new Chinese consumer

The value of China's emerging middle class

Ultimately, China can't hope to unleash the power of its consumers unless the economy creates more jobs and pays higher wages, so regulatory policies must change. Banks should be encouraged to support the services sector as well as small and medium-sized enterprises. Dividend policies for state-owned enterprises should be changed and the development of equity markets encouraged. By 2025, a comprehensive effort to restructure the economy along these lines could add 3.5 to 6.0 percentage points to consumption's share of GDP.

A fundamental shift

China has already embarked on measures that will shift the focus of its economy away from heavy industry and exports and toward services and consumer products. But two wide gaps remain: between what's been proposed and achieved and between what's been achieved and the country's long-term potential. The government's stimulus package, by offsetting collapsed overseas demand for Chinese goods with a huge jolt of new domestic public and business investment, has helped the country shake off the global recession's immediate impact. But the stimulus package does little to tilt the balance in favor of private consumption. In the short term, it will do just the reverse: 89 percent of it is devoted to infrastructure investment, only 8 percent to measures supporting consumption.

The authors wish to acknowledge the contributions of Adam Eichner, Wenkan Liao, and Stefano Negri to the research underlying this article.

Copyright © 2009 McKinsey & Company. All rights reserved.

We welcome your comments on this article. Please send them to quarterly_comments@ mckinsey.com.

A genuine shift away from the old paradigm will require difficult economic and political choices and is sure to meet with opposition. Yet such a shift is undoubtedly in the long-term interest of the nation as a whole. A more consumer-centric economy would allocate capital and resources more efficiently, generate more jobs, spread the benefits of growth more equitably—and grow more rapidly—than China will if it remains on its present course. The narrowing of the trade surplus and the Chinese consumer's larger contribution to global growth would make foreign ties more harmonious. In years past, China has demonstrated a remarkable ability to make major economic changes rapidly in pursuit of broad national objectives. It can do so again by shifting to a new economic paradigm that unleashes the spending power of its consumers. o

Leigh Wells

Leadership lessons for hard times

A series of interviews with 14 CEOs and chairmen of major companies sheds light on the foundations of corporate leadership.

Dennis Carey, Michael Patsalos-Fox, and Michael Useem

During the current global recession, much attention has been devoted to the mistakes that sparked the financial and economic crisis, in hopes of not repeating them. Less has been given to what's been done well amid the turmoil—to learn, for example, how best to lead a company through these tough times.

Dennis Carey is a senior client partner of board and CEO recruiting at Korn/Ferry International, **Michael Patsalos-Fox** is a director in McKinsey's New York office, and **Michael Useem** is the William and Jacalyn Egan Professor of Management and the director of the Center for Leadership and Change Management at the Wharton School of the University of Pennsylvania.

To contribute to that understanding, we interviewed the leaders of 14 major companies (see sidebar "Who's who"), all seasoned CEOs or chairmen, asking them to reflect on what they felt they have learned so far. We were keen not to limit their comments to the current recession and therefore also asked them to consider previous challenges they had faced in a turnaround or a crisis. The companies they lead are in diverse industries, face varied challenges, and have performed quite differently. We are attempting neither to judge their performance nor to draw up a set of rules on how to lead through tough times. Instead, what emerges from the interviews is agreement on some broad principles that can help guide behavior in the executive suite and the boardroom, as well as interactions with employees, customers, and investors.

Confront reality

"Always question whether the 'halo effect' of a business or business situation is blinding you to what lies on the horizon."
—Herbert Henkel, chairman, president, and CEO
of Ingersoll Rand

Few predicted the magnitude of the current crisis. But those in the corporate world who first detected—and accepted—the fact that something was amiss had a distinct advantage in implementing strategies to help weather the storm.

In the summer of 2008, Ingersoll Rand's Herbert Henkel noticed that European orders in the company's transport refrigeration business had slumped, even though business was still booming in other divisions. He was alarmed: a fall in the delivery of perishable foods surely indicated trouble in the supply chain. "I couldn't help thinking, what if that figure really is indicative of what's out ahead? What are we going to do about it?"

Henkel, squaring up to what he detected, forecast zero growth in Europe during the third quarter, though analysts thought he was "nuts." His forecast was wrong: growth fell by 15 percent. Yet Ingersoll Rand got ahead of the curve by quickly putting contingency plans in place, restructuring, and running down inventory. "Of course, we still had to go back and do more," he reflects. "But by not ignoring that one indicator, we did get a head start."

Getting ahead of the curve means taking a hard look at what the future might hold, and that requires a degree of courage. The point made by Henkel and others is how difficult it can be for leaders to take action—and to persuade others to follow their lead—if a business seems to be thriving.

Who's who	Edward Breen	George Buckley	R. Kerry Clark	Jay Fishman
	Chairman and CEO	Chairman, president, and CEO	Chairman and CEO	Chairman and CEO
	Tyco International		**Cardinal Health**	**Travelers**
	Schaffhausen, Switzerland	**3M**	Dublin, Ohio	New York, New York
	Industrial conglomerate	St. Paul, Minnesota *Industrial conglomerate*	*Health care distributor*	*Property and casualty insurance*
			2008 revenue: $91.1 billion	
	2008 revenue: $20.2 billion	**2008 revenue:** $25.3 billion	**2008 employees:** 47,600	**2008 revenue:** $23.8 billion
	2008 employees: 113,000	**2008 employees:** 79,200		**2008 employees:** 33,000

Eight years ago, when Michael Jackson arrived at AutoNation, for example, the auto industry was selling as many as 17 million units a year, but its high fixed costs made him fear what would happen if the economic environment changed. At his first management meeting, he therefore announced his desire to find a business model that would let AutoNation break even, even if the auto industry sold only 10 million units. He also wanted to understand what would have to happen for sales to take such a nosedive and how the business would need to be remodeled to survive. "Everybody looked at me like I had six heads," he recalls. "Eventually, we came to the conclusion that, among other things, it would take a credit crisis to get volumes that low, because in our business, nothing moves without credit. So we got out of the finance and leasing business," says Jackson. "Without the limitation on risk we put in place, we would be in deep, serious trouble at the moment."

CEOs also need courage to make hard decisions quickly. Phil Hildebrand, of HealthMarkets, and Steve Miller, of Delphi, both remarked on the importance of decisiveness to prevent problems from escalating. But it can be hard to achieve in the absence of perfect data. "A lot of CEOs are slow to react, and their problems get away from them," says Edward Breen, of Tyco International. "You have to get as much data as quickly as possible. But you will never get all of it—so you need to make decisions quickly."

Besides courage, staying ahead of the curve entails having the mechanisms and governance models that allow companies to confront realities unimaginably different from those they would ordinarily expect. Monitoring systems that pick up warning signs are important. So too is an environment, both physical and psychological, where alternative interpretations of the signs can be aired and considered with care and interest.

Eric Foss	**Herbert Henkel**	**Phil Hildebrand**	**Michael Jackson**	**A. G. Lafley**
Chairman and CEO	Chairman, president, and CEO	President, director, and CEO	Chairman and CEO	Chairman
Pepsi Bottling Group	**Ingersoll Rand**	**HealthMarkets**	**AutoNation** Fort Lauderdale, Florida *Automotive retailing*	**P&G** Cincinnati, Ohio *Household products*
Somers, New York *Soft drinks*	Dublin, Ireland *Industrial machinery*	North Richland Hills, Texas *Life and health insurance*		
2008 revenue: $13.8 billion	**2008 revenue:** $13.2 billion		**2008 revenue:** $14.1 billion	**2008 revenue:** $83.5 billion
2008 employees: 66,800	**2008 employees:** 60,000	**2008 revenue:** $1.5 billion (2007 est.)	**2008 employees:** 20,000	**2008 employees:** 138,000
		2008 employees: 2,000 (2007 est.)		

At Cardinal Health, Kerry Clark wanted to have a better grasp of such potentially unpleasant realities and felt that historical practice— employees were given forecasts and simply told to meet them—was a hindrance. Instead, he made business leaders accountable for making forecasts and doing everything possible to meet them, while regularly and openly reviewing them. "It's all too easy for a corporate leader to say, 'Don't give me more bad news. Just go fix it,'" muses Clark. "But you have to beat back that kind of attitude and create an atmosphere where people feel they can talk about the forecast, how they can improve it, and what resources they might need." He says that the new system required a cultural change but is yielding results—for instance, revealing problems earlier.

Sysco's Richard Schneiders puts it this way: "You have to be open to diverse points of view. Given the speed of change, I don't know how a business will be able to continue to flourish in the future without being receptive to different points of view."

At board meetings, put strategy center stage
"The board has been heavily involved in strategy formulation with me, and we have a better strategy because of it."
—Bill Nuti, chairman, president, and CEO of NCR

The way CEOs work with their boards has changed fundamentally during the past year. In tough times, difficult decisions must be made quickly, so it's not surprising that many CEOs find themselves communicating more regularly with the board to keep it abreast of developments. Full board meetings have been supplemented by letters, e-mails, intranet postings, informal discussions, and conference calls. At Cardinal Health, "board updates"—conference calls held as frequently as every two weeks—address questions from board members. "They weren't board meetings. There were no minutes. No

Terry Lundgren	Robert S. 'Steve' Miller	Bill Nuti	Richard Schneiders	Ron Sugar
Chairman, president, and CEO	Executive chairman	Chairman, president, and CEO	Chairman and CEO	Chairman and CEO
			Sysco	**Northrop Grumman**
Macy's	**Delphi**	**NCR**	Houston, Texas	Los Angeles,
Cincinnati, Ohio	Troy, Michigan	Dayton, Ohio	*Food distributors*	California
Department stores	*Auto parts and equipment*	*Electronic equipment*		*Shipbuilding and military contracting*
			2008 revenue: $37.5 billion	
2008 revenue: $24.9 billion		**2008 revenue:** $5.3 billion	**2008 employees:** 50,000	**2008 revenue:** $33.9 billion
2008 employees: 167,000	**2008 revenue:** $18.1 billion	**2008 employees:** 22,400		**2008 employees:** 123,600
	2008 employees: 146,600			

one was obliged to attend. But it was very helpful," says Clark, who sees the updates as an efficient way to address individual concerns and increase confidence in the management team.

Many CEOs have already accepted the need for frequent and open communication with their boards, a practice they say proves its worth when difficult decisions must be made. If directors are up to speed, they are better placed to offer both support and advice. What has changed markedly is the content of board discussions. In particular, discussions about strategy are no longer the preserve of a once-a-year off-site meeting. The pace of change—crisis or no crisis—makes that model unworkable.

Today, at many companies, strategy is on the agenda of every board meeting. "The world moves at a pace that requires strategy to be front and center all of the time," says NCR's Bill Nuti. "There are too many variables that come into play in a normal cycle, let alone this one, that can rapidly change the course of your company, so I bring strategy up at every single meeting." Eric Foss, of Pepsi Bottling, decided to integrate strategy into every board meeting at the beginning of 2008, before the crisis. It was a fortunate decision, according to Foss, considering the board's contribution. He, like others, is happy to communicate more frequently with a talented board not just to build its trust but also to benefit from its experience. Several CEOs said that working to get the right people with the right experience onto their boards had been a priority, over the course of several years, for that very reason.

'It's all too easy for a corporate leader to say, "Don't give me more bad news; just go fix it"'

Nuti credits his board with helping him understand the potential magnitude of the current downturn very quickly. "You get great research when you can pull information from board members who all sit on 2 or 3 boards. You're getting the perspective of 18 different boards. I was looking for commonality in their feedback and, fortunately—or unfortunately, in the light of circumstances—there was a lot of commonality."

Be transparent with employees

"The only way to address uncertainty is to communicate and communicate. And when you think you've just about got to everybody, then communicate some more."
        —Terry Lundgren, chairman, president, and CEO of Macy's

One legacy of the current downturn will be a reinforced belief in the value of frequent, transparent communication with employees, and

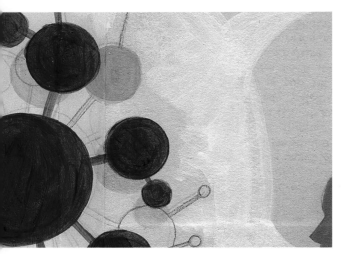

not just the CEO's direct reports. The CEOs we interviewed could not overemphasize the power of openness at all levels.

"At Cardinal, we work hard on internal communications," says Clark. "We do a lot of town hall meetings, for example. We used to just do them around earnings time, but now we do them to discuss any major initiative that's under way." Clark also notes that investor relations (IR) and internal communications work hand in hand, so that any information that goes to the investor community is reworked for employees. "We do a very good job of making sure information doesn't get in front of one group without getting in front of the other."

Being open about what is happening in a company is partly a question of integrity: employees deserve honesty. Openness also builds respect, trust, and solidarity, all of which in turn help employees stay focused on the task of running the business at a time when financial rewards might be limited and the future uncertain (see sidebar "Leaders coping with crisis: Selected McKinsey Global Survey Results"). Openness helps build morale as well. A CEO cannot mislead people and certainly shouldn't panic them, but explaining problems and the actions being taken to deal with them builds confidence in the quality of the CEO's leadership. "People will take any hill, walk into the worst situation, if they have faith in your leadership and know what your strategy and objectives are," says Tyco's Breen.

3M's George Buckley emphasizes, in addition, the need to assure employees that the CEO has faith in them and that they will not be blamed for things beyond their control—such as the state of the economy. "When they're battling the marketplace, they need to know you will support them," he says.

Finally, openness helps ensure that everyone in an organization understands how to make a difference. When the CEO explains "the current situation," says Ingersoll Rand's Henkel, "people understand why we need cash both to pay off debt and to be able to continue making investments. That, for example, makes them think twice about ordering something just to be on the safe side."

Yet although the importance of good internal communication is widely understood, it can slip from the priority list in a crisis. "In hard times, we ask employees to work harder than ever," comments P&G's A. G. Lafley. "But in hard times, you get caught up with investors, analysts, the media, suppliers, and retailers. It's all too easy to overlook your employees at precisely the time you should be communicating more with them."

Be open with investors

"Our policy is: 'If in doubt, communicate.' We always want to conduct our business with integrity and forthrightness."
> —Ron Sugar, chairman and CEO of Northrop Grumman

Most CEOs we interviewed have noticed that the amount of time they spend communicating with investors has risen exponentially of late. Here too they strive to be as open as possible. "If I've learned anything in the last 18 months, it's that transparency in troubled times really matters," says Travelers' Jay Fishman. Yet he believes the crisis has revealed that transparency still goes against the grain for many people. "If asked to describe this or that exposure, the advice from many IR departments is to use some formulation that basically says don't worry. I've tried to resist that. Now is not the time to tell people not to worry. If you're in the financial-services industry, you ought to be able to quantify. I try to be specific, and we've gained credibility as a result." Pepsi's Foss too recommends transparency with investors: "we're facing up to our issues" and in this way "demonstrating that we have a management team that knows what it's doing."

But there are caveats. In times of crisis, there can be a tendency to focus entirely on short-term results—a tendency CEOs should counter. While acknowledging current difficulties, it is just as important to emphasize what is being done to build a company's longer-term health. Fishman, like others, has spent much time talking about his company's mid- and long-term strategy, its efforts to improve productivity, and his willingness to sacrifice some short-term performance to create longer-term value.

There is also a feeling among CEOs that not all investors are equal. While chief executives are acutely aware of disclosure requirements, some say that their companies would gain very little if they spent more time with short-term investors. CEOs count themselves lucky when they feel strategically aligned with long-term investors who have large holdings. That makes these CEOs believe they have some breathing space in a crisis, and as a result they may not have to spend a great deal more time with their investors. But they note how hard they worked to recruit those investors.

When Jackson took over at AutoNation, for instance, he knew that to succeed he would have to attract a new shareholder base prepared to sacrifice some short-term profit for longer-term gain. "The investors

I have now understand the business model, and that's been a huge plus. But it didn't happen by itself," he points out.

Build and protect the culture

"Stay focused on culture, people, and values: it's the area most likely to get compromised in this environment."
—Eric Foss, chairman and CEO of Pepsi Bottling Group

A healthy company enjoys not only strong financials but also a culture and values that bind it together. Much of what our interviewees describe as important is driven by corporate culture—open communication or a focus on a company's long-term health, for example. Several CEOs chose to highlight how a strong culture had helped them in hard times and how important it is not to sacrifice that culture when a company comes under pressure.

Leaders coping with crisis: Selected McKinsey Global Survey Results

Executives around the world are working longer hours, taking on additional responsibilities, and experiencing higher levels of stress as they struggle to address the economic downturn, according to a *McKinsey Quarterly* survey.[1] More surprising, rather than feeling as turbulent as the economy, executives say they feel relatively stable and content about their companies, their work, and their performance as business leaders since the crisis began. All is not well, though. Beyond the averages—and the executive suites—middle managers report dramatically lower levels of contentment than do their more senior colleagues, as well as less of a desire to stay with their current employers.

Most executives are coping fairly well with the potentially stressful effects of the crisis: more than 50 percent say stress levels have increased but are manageable in the long term. However, one in five executives say they are worried about coping with the increased stress levels going forward.

Middle managers differ from senior executives in the sources and degree of stress they identify (exhibit). In addition, more than half say they have taken on additional responsibilities

without a promotion, which may help to explain why they are more disconnected from their companies. Indeed, 27 percent of middle managers—compared with 18 percent of all executives—say they find their current roles less meaningful and exciting than their roles were before the crisis. And just 36 percent of middle managers—compared with 52 percent of all executives—report that they are very or extremely likely to choose to be with their current employers two years from now, given their current excitement about their roles and their companies as well as their current stress levels.

Despite this dissonance, it is notable that around 80 percent of all the executives we surveyed find their current roles equally or more meaningful now than they did before the crisis and are at least somewhat likely to stay with their employers.

[1] *McKinsey Quarterly* conducted the survey in July 2009 and received responses from a worldwide representative sample of 1,653 executives. Of these respondents, 47 percent are C-level executives or corporate directors, 33 percent are senior executives, and 18 percent are middle managers. (Note that these figures do not sum to 100 percent, because of rounding.)

The contributors to the development and analysis of this survey include **Kevin Lane,** a principal in McKinsey's Zurich office, and **Monica McGurk,** a principal in the Atlanta office.

Jackson says that the most critical battle he waged when he arrived at AutoNation was destroying the "growth at any cost" culture. "We wanted entrepreneurialism, but we also wanted the highest standards of integrity," he says. Over the next three years, he worked hard to nurture and recruit the right people for the company's top 350 positions and to purge the "high-performing money makers whose risk profile would keep you awake at night." This amounted, he says, to a cultural revolution that has delivered a sustainable competitive advantage—and one that he isn't about to jeopardize by shedding his best talent.

Lafley too feels that the culture he worked hard to build at the beginning of the decade at P&G has paid off. Concerned that the company had become too inward looking, he flipped that around. "Take trust. We only ever talked about it in relation to employees. But what matters

Exhibit 1: **Personal concerns on the back burner**
Considering possible ways that the economic crisis might affect you or your company, which of the following ways, if any, are most stressful for you in your work?

% of respondents whose physical and mental stress has increased because of the crisis,[1] n = 1,653

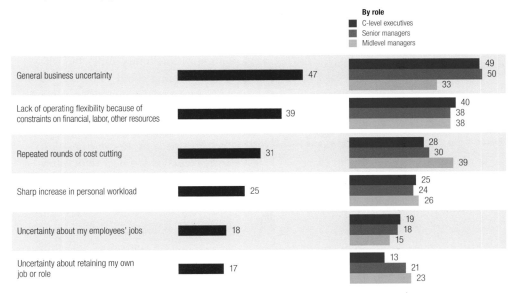

[1]Respondents who answered "other" or "don't know" are not shown; full list of responses not shown.

The full results of this survey, 'Leaders in the crisis: McKinsey Global Survey Results,' are available on mckinseyquarterly.com/surveys.

most now is that consumers trust our brand, that shareholders trust our stock, that customers trust us to be the best supplier, and that suppliers trust us to be their best customer."

At Travelers, Fishman is proud of the culture he has nurtured, which rewards returns on capital rather than revenue and has offered some protection during the financial crisis. "We never criticize anyone for a transaction not done, not ever—not ever," he says.

Keep faith with the future

"If you don't invest in the future and don't plan for the future, there won't be one."

> —George Buckley, chairman, president, and CEO of 3M

CEOs and their leadership teams need to remain forward looking despite the near-term pressures their businesses might be facing. There are opportunities in a crisis, even though that notion is too lightly bandied around when companies and their employees come under real stress. Many of the CEOs we interviewed were determined to ensure that their companies emerge from this recession with a competitive advantage by setting the course for higher productivity, acquiring a footprint in a new market, or not squandering a company's talent or reputation in pursuit of lower costs.

Likewise, at P&G, Lafley continues to look for growth opportunities through alliances and acquisitions and is increasing the company's investment in R&D and innovation. His efforts require resolve. "We're keeping the pedal to the metal on innovation, for example, but it's not always easy when people are complaining about your short-term profit performance. You have to get the balance right between the present and the future, but we want to come out of this recession stronger than when we went in," he declares.

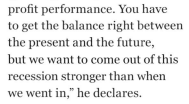

Nuti too acknowledges the difficulty of looking to the future while concentrating on a challenging present. When he arrived at NCR, in 2005, he was concerned that although the company was rightly focused on cost cutting to regain profitability, it had no plan for the future. "My challenge, up to and including the last six to eight months, has been to keep driving the transformation of the company while still adapting to the realities of the present. You can't cut the things that will impact your ability to reach your vision." Nuti suggests using a scalpel rather than an ax.

The ax will make the biggest dent on costs and make you look smart for a while. But the more precise scalpel can protect a company's future, even if there are fewer short-term gains.

●   ●   ●

Copyright © 2009 McKinsey & Company. All rights reserved.

We welcome your comments on this article. Please send them to quarterly_comments@ mckinsey.com.

None of the CEOs we interviewed claimed to have attempted anything revolutionary. What was evident, however, was their resolve in pursuing the principles they thought were right, often in the face of opposition. Leadership becomes increasingly important in tough times, when so much is at risk—but it can be even harder to exercise. The leadership "musts" described in this article have made the greatest difference for these CEOs on the front line. ○

Center Stage

A look at current trends and topics in management

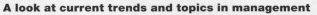

Increasing the energy efficiency of supply chains

Tobias A. Meyer

Tobias Meyer is an associate principal in McKinsey's Frankfurt office.

Supply chains have become increasingly global over the latter half of the century, as the globalization of trade was fueled by cheap oil. Today, the transportation of goods consumes 15 million barrels of oil a day— roughly one-fifth of total production.

In a study of energy efficiency in supply chains, McKinsey looked at numerous opportunities to reduce the amount of oil used to get goods from a manufacturer's dock to a retailer's shelf. These opportunities are available not only to manufacturers but also to wholesalers, distributors, carriers, and third-party businesses. We grouped these opportunities into six levers to illustrate possible next steps and

Potential opportunities for reducing energy consumption, six levers

Supply chain set up

Lever 1	Lever 2	Lever 3
Increase value density (product's economic value vs its weight/volume) For example, limit filler materials or excess packaging	**Reduce average transportation distance** For example, use several distribution centers instead of one	**Change the mix of transportation modes** For example, shift from use of truck to rail

Reduction in energy consumption per unit vs 2007 base, by scenario, %

Scenario A: Oil at $40 a barrel

Scenario B: Oil at $100 a barrel

Scenario C: Oil at $250 a barrel

Lever 1: −2 −3 −3

Lever 2: −1 −4 −15

Lever 3: −3 −4 −7

For example, in lever 3 the energy efficiency of different modes of transportation varies widely, as does the potential for improvement. Air freight and trucking consume a greater proportion of energy relative to capacity than do ocean shipping or rail. Shifting the mix of transportation modes from the former to the latter has the potential to make a major impact on energy consumption.

examined potential gains in supply chain energy efficiency under three scenarios (Scenarios A, B, and C), based on low, medium, and high oil prices and electricity costs. Potential reductions in energy intensity (amount of energy used per unit of transport activity; for example, metric ton kilometers) could reach as high as 38 percent in Scenario B by 2020.

For a more detailed look at the six levers, see the interactive presentation on mckinseyquarterly.com.

Transport assets

Lever 4	Lever 5	Lever 6
Address asset technology	**Assess usage of individual assets**	**Assess usage of collective assets**
For example, increase average size of transport vessels	For example, use route planning to manage time lost in traffic	For example, upgrade infrastructure, such as berthing capacity

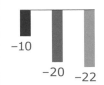

−10

−20 −22

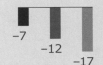

−7

−12

−17

−1   −2   −3

For example, in lever 4 there are substantial opportunities to improve the energy efficiency of transportation assets. Some factors are more relevant than one might think. Scale, for example, is an often-underestimated driver of energy efficiency in transportation. Typically, the doubling in capacity of a transport asset increases its energy efficiency by some 25 percent.

How sustainability programs create value

In the past, companies have often struggled to justify investing in social responsibility programs. Yet today, many businesses are creating real value through their environmental, social, and governance activities.

These articles offer suggestions on how businesses can fulfill their contract with society *and* improve their bottom line.

Don Kilpatrick

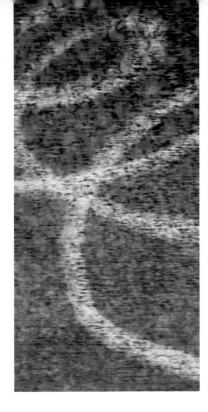

Corporate Finance

Valuing social responsibility programs

Most companies see corporate social responsibility programs as a way to fulfill the contract between business and society. But do they create financial value?

Sheila Bonini, Timothy M. Koller, and Philip H. Mirvis

Companies face increasing pressure from governments, competitors, and employees to play a leading role in addressing a wide array of environmental, social, and governance issues—ranging from climate change to obesity to human rights—in a company's supply chain. Over the past 30 years, most of them have responded by developing corporate social responsibility or sustainability initiatives to fulfill their contract with society by addressing such issues.

Gathering the data needed to justify sustained, strategic investments in such programs can be difficult, but without this information executives and investors often see programs as separate from a company's core business or unrelated to its shareholder value. Some companies have made great progress tracking operational metrics (such as tons of carbon emitted) or social indicators (say, the number of students enrolled in programs) but often have difficulty linking such metrics and indicators to a real financial impact. Others insist that the effects of such programs are either too indirect to value or too deeply embedded in the core business to be measured meaningfully: for example, it can be very hard to separate the financial impact of offering healthier products from the impact of other aspects of the brand, such as quality and price.

Sheila Bonini is a consultant in McKinsey's Silicon Valley office, and Tim Koller is a principal in the New York office; Philip Mirvis is a senior research fellow at Boston College's Center for Corporate Citizenship.

Yet many companies are creating real value through their environmental, social, and governance activities—through increased sales,
decreased costs, or reduced risks—and some have developed hard
data to measure even the long-term and indirect value of environmental, social, and governance programs (see sidebar, "About
the research"). It's not surprising that the best of them create financial value in ways the market already assesses—growth, return
on capital, risk management, and quality of management (Exhibit 1).

How environmental, social, and governance programs create value

The most widely known way that environmental, social, and governance programs create value is by enhancing the reputations of
companies—their stakeholders' attitudes about their tangible actions—
and respondents to a recent McKinsey survey agree.[1]

Moreover, it has long been clear that financially valuable objectives
may depend, at least in part, on a company's reputation for environmental, social, and governance programs that meet community needs
and go beyond regulatory requirements or industry norms. However,
environmental, social, and governance programs can create value in
many other ways that support growth, improve returns on capital,
reduce risk, or improve management quality. Breaking out the value of
these activities enables companies to communicate it to investors and
financial professionals.

About the research

To better understand the relationship between
environmental, social, and governance
activities and value creation, we surveyed 238
CFOs, investment professionals, and finance
executives from a full range of industries
and regions. The survey was conducted in
conjunction with a survey of 127 corporate
social responsibility and sustainability
professionals and self-described socially
responsible institutional investors that were
reached through the Boston College Center for
Corporate Citizenship. Both surveys were in the
field in December of 2008. To get a bottom-up
view, we also constructed case studies of
20 companies with leading environmental,
social, and governance programs in a number
of industries.

Growth

Our case studies highlighted five areas in which these
programs have a demonstrable impact on growth.

New markets. IBM has used environmental, social,
and governance programs to establish its presence
in new markets. For example, the company uses
its Small and Medium Enterprise (SME) Toolkit to
develop a track record with local stakeholders,
including government officials and nongovernmen-
tal organizations (NGOs). In partnership with
the World Bank's International Finance Corporation,
India's ICICI Bank, Banco Real (Brazil), and Dun
& Bradstreet Singapore, IBM is using the service to
provide free Web-based resources on business
management to small and midsize enterprises in
developing economies. Overall, there are 30 SME
Toolkit sites, in 16 languages. Helping to build such
businesses not only improves IBM's reputation

---

[1] See "Valuing corporate social responsibility: McKinsey Global Survey Results,"
mckinseyquarterly.com, February 2009.

Exhibit 1: **Quantifiable value**

Environmental, social, and governance (ESG) programs create value in each of the metrics the market typically uses. These contributions extend beyond the obvious effect of building a good reputation.

Here are selected examples.

Growth	Access to new markets through exposure from ESG programs	Returns on capital	Bottom-line cost savings through environmental operations and practices
	Innovation/new products in response to unmet social needs		Higher employee morale; lower turnover or recruitment costs
Risk management	Lower level of risk by complying with regulations and demands of nongovernmental organizations	Management quality	Leadership development through employees' participation in ESG programs
	Sustainable supply chain enabled by engaging in community development		Ability to adapt to changing political/ social situations by engaging local communities

and relationships in new markets but also helps it to develop relationships with companies that could become future customers.

New products. IBM has also developed green data-center products, which help the company grow by offering products that meet customers' environmental concerns. A new collaboration between IBM and the Nature Conservancy, for example, is developing 3D-imaging technology to help advance efforts to improve water quality. This project applies IBM's existing capability in sensors that can communicate wirelessly with a central data-management system in order to provide decision makers with summaries that improve water management. At the same time, it also addresses an important environmental need—and creates a new business opportunity for IBM.

New customers. Telefónica has been developing new products and services geared to customers over the age of 60. To help overcome what the company calls a "knowledge barrier," it has collaborated with associations for older people in an effort to introduce retired men and women to the benefits of new technologies—for example, teaching them to communicate with grandchildren living abroad. The company meets a social need by helping this population use modern technologies and services while building a customer base in an under-penetrated market.

Market share. Coca-Cola has shown how a company can use enlightened environmental practices to increase its sales. Its new eKO-freshment coolers, vending machines, and soda fountains are far more environmentally friendly than the ones they replaced: they not

only eliminate the use of hydrofluorocarbons (greenhouse gases) as
a refrigerant but also have a sophisticated energy-management device
that Coca-Cola developed to reduce the energy these machines
consume. Together, these innovations increase the equipment's energy
efficiency by up to 35 percent. The company highlights the benefits
to retailers—especially the financial savings from energy efficiency—
and requests prime space in their outlets in return for providing
more efficient systems.

Innovation. Dow Chemical has committed itself to achieving, by 2015, at
least three breakthroughs in four areas: an affordable and adequate
food supply, decent housing, sustainable water supplies, or improved
personal health and safety. All have a connection to an existing or
planned Dow business. The company has already made progress in its
Breakthroughs to World Challenges initiative, for example, by uti-
lizing its understanding of plastics and water purification to supplement
its venture capital investment and loan guarantee support to a social
entrepreneur in India who has developed an inexpensive community-
based water filtration system. The initiative's ultimate goal is a new
business model to sell new products at reasonable prices, meeting social
needs while contributing to Dow's bottom line.

Returns on capital

We have seen companies generate returns on capital from their
environmental, social, and governance programs in several ways—
most often through operational efficiency and workforce efficiency.

Operational efficiency. These programs can help companies realize substantial savings by meeting environmental goals—for instance,
reducing energy costs through energy efficiency, reducing input costs
through packaging initiatives, and improving processes. Such
efficiencies often require upfront capital investments to upgrade technologies, systems, and products, but returns can be substantial.

Novo Nordisk's proactive stance on environmental issues, for
example, has improved its operational efficiency. In 2006, the company set an ambitious goal: reducing its carbon dioxide emissions
by 10 percent in ten years. In partnership with a local energy supplier,
Novo Nordisk has identified and realized energy savings at its
Danish production sites, which account for 85 percent of the company's
global carbon dioxide emissions. It uses the savings to pay the
supplier's premium price for wind power. In three years, the effort
has eliminated 20,000 tons of carbon dioxide emissions, and by
2014 green electricity will power all of the company's activities in
Denmark. In this way, Novo Nordisk is not only reducing its emissions, increasing the energy efficiency of its operations, and cutting
its costs but also helping to build Denmark's market for renew-
able energy.

Workforce efficiency. Best Buy has undertaken a targeted effort to reduce employee turnover, particularly among women. In 2006, it launched the Women's Leadership Forum (WoLF), which shows groups of female employees how they can help the company to innovate by generating ideas, implementing them, and measuring the results. These innovations—which largely involve enhancing the customer experience for women by altering the look and feel of Best Buy stores and modifying their product assortment—have significantly boosted sales to women without decreasing sales to men. Besides fostering innovation, the program helps women to create their own corporate support networks and encourages them to build leadership skills by organizing events that benefit their communities. In the program's first two years, turnover among women decreased by more than 5 percent annually.

Risk management

Companies often see environmental, social, and governance issues as potential risks, and many programs in these areas were originally designed to mitigate them—particularly risks to a company's reputation but also, for example, problems with regulation, gaining the public support needed to do business, and ensuring the sustainability of supply chains. Today, companies manage many of these risks by taking stands on questions ranging from corruption and fraud to data security and labor practices. Creating and complying with such policies is an extremely important part of risk management, though one that isn't likely to be a source of significant differentiation. But leading companies *can* differentiate themselves by going beyond the basics and taking a proactive role in managing environmental, social, and governance risks. Such an approach can have an important and positive financial impact, since negative environmental, social, and governance events can have significant potential cost.

Regulation. In most geographies, regulatory policy shapes the structure and conduct of industries and can dramatically affect corporate profits, sometimes dwarfing gains from ordinary operational measures.[2] It is therefore critically important for companies to manage their regulatory agenda proactively—ideally, by having a seat at the table when regulations for their industries are contemplated and crafted. To build the necessary trust with regulators and to secure a voice in the ongoing discussion, it helps to have solid relationships with stakeholders and a reputation for strong performance on environmental, social, and governance issues.

Verizon, for instance, very actively manages its relationships with stakeholders and strives to establish regular contacts and strong ties

[2] See Scott C. Beardsley, Luis Enriquez, and Robin Nuttall, "Managing regulation in a new era," mckinseyquarterly.com, December 2008.

with policy makers. To help formulate sound—and favorable—energy and climate policies, the company has also sponsored research on the way information communications technology promotes energy efficiency. They sponsored the research behind the *Smart 2020*[3] report, for example, which explains in detail how this technology, together with broadband Internet connections, can help the United States to reduce carbon emissions by 22 percent and reliance on foreign oil by 36 percent by no later than 2020.

Public support. To operate in a country or business, companies need a modicum of public support, particularly on sensitive issues. Coca-Cola, for example, has been proactive in identifying the risks to its business posed by water access, availability, and quality. In 2003, Coca-Cola began developing a risk-assessment model to measure water risks at the plant level, such as supply reliability, watersheds, social issues, economics, compliance, and efficiency. The model helped Coca-Cola to quantify the potential risks and consequently enabled the company to put sufficient resources into developing and implementing plans to mitigate those risks. It now has a global water strategy in place that includes attention to plant performance, watershed protection, sustainable water for communities, and building global awareness. Their actions help avoid potential backlash over water usage as well as potential operational issues from water shortages.

Supply chains. Some companies have moved beyond focusing on the risks from the day-to-day practices of their suppliers and now consider the suppliers' long-term sustainability as well. Under Nestlé's Creating Shared Value strategy, for instance, a business has to make sense for all its stakeholders. As an example, Nestlé works directly with the farmers and agricultural communities that supply about 40 percent of its milk and 10 percent of its coffee. To ensure its direct and privileged access to these communities, Nestlé promotes their development by building infrastructure, training farmers, and paying fair market prices directly to producers rather than middlemen. In return, the company receives higher-quality agricultural ingredients for its products. These strong relationships also give Nestlé's factories a reliable source of supply, even when the overall market runs short. When the price of milk powder soared in 2007, for example, Nestlé's direct links to farmers mitigated its supply and price risks in certain parts of the world and protected the interests of all stakeholders—from farmers to consumers.

Management quality

CFOs and professional investors often see high-performing environmental, social, and governance programs as a proxy for the effectiveness

[3] *SMART 2020: Enabling the Low Carbon Economy in the Information Age*, The Climate Group and the Global eSustainability Initiative (GeSI), 2008.

of a company's management. They may be onto something. In our observation, these programs can have a strong impact in all three areas that investors typically consider important: leadership strength and development, both at the top and through the ranks; the overall adaptability of a business; and the balance between short-term priorities and a long-term strategic view.

Leadership development. IBM's Corporate Service Corps sends top-ranked rising leaders to work pro bono with NGOs, entrepreneurs, and government agencies in strategic emerging markets. The program has already improved the leadership skills of its participants in a statistically significant way; raised their cultural intelligence, global awareness, and commitment to IBM; and given the company new knowledge and skills. In a recent evaluation, nearly all participants indicated that their involvement with the corps increased the likelihood that they would stay at IBM.

Adaptability. Companies flexible enough to meet unforeseen challenges—for instance, by remaining in countries or communities during times of crisis or conflict—often reap long-term benefits, such as strong relationships and credibility with local communities. Environmental, social, and governance programs are one way to boost this kind of resiliency. Cargill, for example, is currently maintaining its presence and operations in Zimbabwe under difficult conditions; instead of paying its local employees in the country's very unstable currency, it compensates them with food parcels and fuel vouchers. The company makes similar long-term investments in local communities in the other 66 countries where it operates.

A long-term strategic view. Companies that take a long-term view use environmental, social, and governance activities to anticipate risks from emerging issues and to turn those risks into opportunities. Novo Nordisk, for instance, manages itself according to principles of a triple bottom line—an economically viable, environmentally sound, and socially responsible approach to business. The company, for example, has not only made investments to prevent, diagnose, and treat diabetes and to build up the related health care infrastructure but has also used these investments to strengthen its position in mature markets and to develop its business in new ones.

Assessing value
Although many executives and investors believe that much of the impact of environmental, social, and governance programs is long term and indirect—and thus nearly impossible to measure—our research suggests otherwise. The impact of environmental programs, for example, can often be measured quickly with traditional business metrics such as cost efficiency. Companies that understand the pathways to value and identify the short- and long-term

effects of these programs will succeed in defining a few targeted metrics to assess them (Exhibit 2).

One such company, Telefónica, having found that its customers' purchasing decisions and loyalty are driven in part by perceptions of its environmental, social, and governance activities, decided to integrate the results of an annual reputation survey into its business strategy. Since then, Telefónica has identified its reputation short-falls, aligned its business strategy with efforts to close them, created action plans to improve its reputation (for instance, by developing new products and services or adapting existing ones), and monitored any improvement. This approach has helped the company to improve its reputation, and the corresponding sales, in a significant way. An internal study shows that in 2006 and 2007, 11 percent of the change in the financial performance of the company reflected changes in its reputation.

UnitedHealth is another company that has assessed the impact of its environmental, social, and governance work. Its social responsi-bility dashboard includes metrics for workplace engagement, ethics, and integrity; supplier diversity; environmental impact; employee–community involvement; stakeholders' perspectives on social

---

Exhibit 2: **Direct and indirect dividends**

Campbell Soup tracked the effects on business drivers of its partnership with the American Heart Association. This analysis revealed the financial impact of their environmental, social, and governance (ESG) programs.

	Effect of ESG programs	Financial impact	
Food and beverage innovation	New products	Direct	Increased sales
Access to and relationships with retailers	New sales opportunities with current retailers; access to new retailers	Direct	Increased sales
	Stronger relationships with current retailers	Indirect	Goodwill
Brand portfolios and brand loyalty	New customers and stronger consumer loyalty	Direct	Increased sales
	Better brand awareness, preference, and image	Indirect	Goodwill
Relationships with consumers and influencers	New sales opportunities created through trusting partnerships	Indirect	Goodwill
	Lower risk of attack from vocal representatives of nongovernmental organizations (NGOs)	Indirect	Goodwill

Source: Interviews with Campbell Soup executives; McKinsey analysis

responsibility; and community giving. All of these metrics track the company's progress in meeting its social mission: helping people live healthier lives. Currently, UnitedHealth's board and senior executives use the dashboard to measure the company's performance and to guide discussions on future priorities, programs, resources, and results. In the future, the dashboard will be made available to customers and other public audiences to demonstrate the company's environmental, social, and governance commitments and progress.

Related articles on mckinseyquarterly.com

Rebuilding corporate reputations

The trust gap between consumers and corporations

When social issues become strategic

• • •

The authors wish to thank Noémie Brun, Thomas Herbig, and Michelle Rosenthal for their contributions to this research.

Copyright © 2009 McKinsey & Company. All rights reserved.

We welcome your comments on this article. Please send them to quarterly_comments@mckinsey.com.

Companies need broad legitimacy in the societies where they operate if they are to sustain their long-term ability to create shareholder value. Equally important, society depends upon big business to provide critical economic and other benefits. This relationship forms the basis of an overarching contract between business and society. Over the past few years, responses to the social, environmental, and governance concerns of politicians, regulators, lawyers, and consumers have reshaped the core businesses of major companies in many sectors: agribusiness, chemicals, fast food, mining, oil, pharmaceuticals, and tobacco, to name just a few. As the social contract has come under more and more pressure, companies are realizing that they just can't ignore environmental, social, and governance issues.○

This article has been adapted from "Valuing corporate social responsibility and sustainability," an essay published by the Boston College Center for Corporate Citizenship in March 2009.

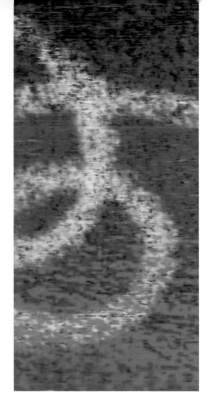

When sustainability means more than green

Protecting the natural environment isn't the whole story: companies must consider their social, economic, and cultural impact as well.

Adam Werbach

Adam Werbach is the CEO of Saatchi & Saatchi S. He is a former president of the Sierra Club and the author of many works on sustainability, including the 1997 book *Act Now, Apologize Later.*

Of the world's 100 largest economic entities, 63 are corporations, not countries. Great power creates great expectations: society increasingly holds global businesses accountable as the only institutions strong enough to meet the huge long-term challenges facing our planet. Coming to grips with them is more than a corporate responsibility—it's essential for corporate survival.

Unfortunately, short-term thinking is now endemic to business strategy. By the time of the great petroleum price spike of 2008, for example, America's Big Three had an advantage over their foreign competitors only in light trucks and SUVs—precisely the cars that consumers didn't want. The possibility of such a firestorm has been obvious for decades, yet the automakers are only now trying to deal with it. For them and all other organizations, survival isn't a right. To endure in a changeable world with more limits on resources and less credit, companies must develop and execute a strategy for sustainability. But that doesn't mean a green strategy. Sustainability is much bigger because it takes into account every dimension of the business environment: social, economic, and cultural, as well as natural.

Until the 1980s, business leaders used the word *sustainability* to mean a company's ability to increase its earnings steadily. The term became widely used in its present sense in 1987, after it appeared in a UN report by Norway's former prime minister Gro Harlem Brundtland, who defined sustainable development as "meeting the needs of the present without compromising the ability of future generations to meet their own needs." More recently, as Michael Pollan, the author of *The Omnivore's Dilemma*, writes, the whole idea has been "in danger of floating away on a sea of inoffensiveness. Everybody, it seems, is for it whatever 'it' means."[1] Sustainability even has a dark side: "greenwashing"—that is, focusing more on communicating your green efforts than on the efforts themselves.

For my purposes, a sustainable business means a business that can thrive in the long term. Sustainability is bigger than a PR stunt or a green product line, bigger even than a heartfelt but occasional nod to ongoing efforts to save the planet. Imagined and implemented fully, sustainability drives a bottom-line strategy to save costs, a top-line strategy to reach a new consumer base, and a talent strategy to get, keep, and develop creative employees. True sustainability has four equal components:

- *social*, to address conditions that affect us all, including poverty, violence, injustice, education, public health, and labor and human rights

- *economic*, to help people and businesses meet their economic needs; for people: securing food, water, shelter, and creature comforts; for businesses: turning a profit

- *environmental*, to protect and restore the earth—for example, by controlling climate change, preserving natural resources, and preventing waste

- *cultural*, to protect and value the diversity through which communities manifest their identity and cultivate traditions across generations

Although the challenges to sustainability are acute, there has never been a better time than the present for a company to play a critical role in helping to resolve them while building up its business. Many of the social and environmental trends we face are sad, even tragic, but sustainability isn't about throwing your business down the drain and embracing your inner saint. That's one reason for looking beyond

[1] Michael Pollan, "Our decrepit food factories," *New York Times*, December 16, 2007.

the green aspects of sustainability and using its social, economic, and cultural sides as tools for building successful companies. Green businesses, green jobs, and emerging green economies will be a central part of the new world now being born, but green alone isn't a broad enough platform to sustain most businesses for the long haul. Those that take into account broader social issues will be better able to thrive and to lead.

A company that aims to achieve greater sustainability must therefore articulate a "North Star goal": a strategic direction that embodies a global human challenge larger than any organization. Such a goal should be consistent with the strengths of the company, have a connection to its core business, and elicit the personal contributions and passions of its members. Finally, the goal ought to be optimistic and aspirational but not impossible—achievable, incrementally, within 5 to 15 years. Like a Christopher Columbus, you as the leader must point to a destination, even though at the start of the journey you may have no idea how to reach it. Your people will figure out how to cast off, when to shift sails, and what to do to move the organization forward.

The stories of two companies, method and Seventh Generation, show how these ideas play out in actual organizations.

Method

The household products company method, based in San Francisco, may be the most successful example of a sustainable business. Using a "cradle to cradle" process—pioneered by Michael Braungart and William McDonough—to develop its products, method ensures that every ingredient of a product is nontoxic and energy efficient throughout its manufacture, use, and disposal. The company considers the past, the present, and the future of all its products by asking if they came from a sustainable source (past), are nontoxic (present), and will be reusable or recyclable (future).

Founded in 2001 by Adam Lowry and Eric Ryan, method quickly achieved $100 million in sales thanks to wide distribution through retailers such as Target. Its line of products extends from hand soaps to laundry detergents to cleaning sprays. All of its products are recyclable, and a large portion of them incorporate recycled content. Yet the company doesn't label itself solely as a green brand. "Green is one aspect of method," said Lowry. "There is tremendous pressure on environmentally conscious businesses to make green their primary message," he added. "But you need to be relevant to a wide audience, and leading with a single green message may exclude new consumers." A brand needs unique qualities, and green won't be unique for long. Eventually, competitive pressures, commodity costs, or regulation will make all products nontoxic, energy efficient, and sustainably packaged, so greenness alone won't be distinctive. To truly be sustainable, a product needs more than just the environmental aspects of quality.

Yet method hardly ignores the environment. Within the walls of the company's headquarters, near San Francisco's Chinatown, visitors can easily see why it describes itself as deep green on the inside. Lowry's job title is chief greenskeeper, and his role is to form and maintain the principles that govern the company. One of them is that it shouldn't use any product that hasn't been proved safe. Lowry keeps a list of "dirty" chemicals (such as ammonia, bleach, and phthalates) that method won't use in any of its products. Because it has yet to find what it considers a nonhazardous antimicrobial agent, for example, it doesn't make antimicrobial products, such as antibacterial hand wash. The company also has a "clean list" of ingredients safe for people and the environment. Small teams of "green chefs" use these ingredients to create products.

An organization so focused on saving resources faces an ongoing challenge to reconcile design, efficacy, and environmental considerations. Method, for example, could reduce the amount of plastic in some of its bottles by 5 percent, but the company believes that a bottle's design is important for the brand and that occasionally it takes 5 percent more plastic to make a beautiful bottle. Sustainability isn't the only goal of the company's design ethos—aesthetics also plays an important role—but method ensures that, so far as possible, the plastic it uses is recyclable and recycled.

The use of plastics involves another hard choice. Most products have dyes, which green consumer circles condemn as evil. Method, however, looks at the dyes and the product as a whole—the dyes on the bottle and those in the liquid. Life cycle analysis of dyes, in Lowry's view, shows that it's much better to put them in liquids than in bottles. Take, for example, method's all-purpose cleaner, sold in a clear container made of 100 percent recycled polyethylene terephthalate (PET). The liquid inside is colored with 0.007 percent of a synthetic purple dye. But Lowry argues that "it's completely degradable and nontoxic. It's a good dye."

A white PET bottle, by contrast, may never get recycled. When white PET gets sorted in municipal-recycling programs, the operators frequently think it's high-density polyethylene (HDPE), the stuff used to make laundry bottles, and send it to the HDPE reprocessor. There it gets punted out as an impurity and sent to landfill. "If you're going to want to tint a PET bottle white, you'll use a thousand times as much dye to dye the bottle and you're going to make it less recyclable," Lowry said. "We want a plastic bottle that will be recycled—not just capable of being recycled."

6:10 · Embed · E-mail

Watch a video interview with Adam Werbach, in which he discusses how businesses can set up a strategy for sustainability, on mckinseyquarterly.com.

Seventh Generation

People have a strong, intimate connection to the household products they use. Perhaps that's why I'm fascinated by the way companies such as Clorox, method, and P&G are riding the new wave of consumer interest in sustainable products. But unlike these relative newcomers, Seventh Generation, a company based in Vermont, started producing them long before they became trendy.

Seventh Generation got its name from the teachings of the Native American Iroquois confederacy: "In our every deliberation, we must consider the impact of our decisions on the next seven generations." The company, founded in 1988 by Jeffrey Hollender, its "chief inspired protagonist," is widely respected as a leading sustainable producer of household products. For more than a decade before new entrants began to compete in this space, Seventh Generation built a loyal following among consumers who want to make a difference through the products they buy.

The company's global imperatives—North Star goals, to use my terminology—connect the operations of the business with the aspirations expressed in its name. These imperatives address a basic question that all executives should ask themselves: what can my company do that the world needs most? Seventh Generation's imperatives hold that all businesses should help everyone who works for them to develop as people and approach everything they do from a systems perspective: a world that is endlessly interconnected, in which everything we do affects everything else. The imperatives also commit the company to ensuring that natural resources are used at a rate that is always below their rate of depletion. The core of Seventh Generation's ethos is the belief that the company can change society and the way other companies work by succeeding in its own business. Forty years of organizational-development research shows that this simple idea attracts high-performance employees and permanently infatuated customers.

Of course, Hollender isn't your typical executive. For example, he eventually plans to transfer his company over to its employees. He gives away corporate secrets by actively blogging. And he made one decision that might have cost the company millions of dollars: until Wal-Mart Stores started its sustainability initiative, he refused to sell products to the giant retailer because he didn't want to be involved with an institution that wasn't actively working to improve its social and environmental performance. When Wal-Mart embraced sustainability, he spent many long hours at the company's headquarters, in Bentonville, Arkansas, sharing his experience with its leaders.

As a pioneer in the category and a person disposed to generosity, Hollender has reacted in a very interesting way, as nearly every major consumer-packaged-goods company started to claim an interest in sustainability. For the most part, he is thrilled, pointing to these other companies as proof that his dream of changing the world is coming true. He worries, though, about greenwashing and the possibility that it will make consumers doubt all products, including Seventh Generation's. "A company that proclaims its commitment to social and environmental responsibility in a clumsy or inauthentic way quickly breeds cynicism and distrust—and invites the inevitable backlash," he said.

Related articles on mckinseyquarterly.com

Helping 'green' products grow

Using energy more efficiently: An interview with the Rocky Mountain Institute's Amory Lovins

Investing in sustainability: An interview with Al Gore and David Blood

Hollender has seen many fellow entrepreneurs sell their companies to larger conglomerates. "Massive buyouts, minimal buy-in," is how he described such transactions, which, he adds, "often act as a fig leaf for large corporations hoping to appropriate the virtues of the ethical company so as to rehabilitate their image." He remains hopeful, however. Meanwhile, he enjoys driving his business from the fringe to the center.

Copyright © 2009 Adam Werbach.

We welcome your comments on this article. Please send them to quarterly_comments@ mckinsey.com.

●   ●   ●

Every crisis is an opportunity. The crisis we face now is our chance—your chance—to build a strategy for sustainability into the core of your company and your life. Such a strategy is a necessity, not an idealistic illusion. ○

This article is adapted from Strategy for Sustainability: A Business Manifesto. *Reprinted by permission of Harvard Business School Press.*

McKinsey conversations with global leaders

James Manyika

John Chambers has a vision of Management 2.0. As CEO and chairman of Cisco Systems, the self-described former "command and control guy" is now harnessing the concepts behind Web 2.0—collaboration and networks—to reshape the organizational and leadership structure of Cisco itself. From social communities and councils to Chambers's own video blogging, the company is riding the next technology wave as much internally as it is externally. Chambers sat down at Cisco's headquarters, in San Jose, to talk with McKinsey's James Manyika about taking advantage of the economic downturn and his approach to decentralized management.

The *Quarterly*: *What have been the hardest lessons you've learned about how to survive, innovate, and break through during a downturn?*

John Chambers: As tough as this downturn is, this is the time when you have a chance to make change. And, while I always wish we had avoided it, how you handle what we call market transitions—and part of that is economic challenges—determines where you are in the future. And unfortunately, the more disruptive they are, actually, the more opportunity they offer. First lesson is—make no mistake about it—while we sound like we move fast, we are very disciplined on how we move. There are rules for an economic downturn. The first is, be realistic: how much did the macroenvironment cause, and how much

James Manyika is a director in McKinsey's San Francisco office.

John Chambers
Chairman and CEO of Cisco Systems

This interview is the first in our new video series *McKinsey conversations with global leaders*, which aims to explore vital management issues, industry insights, and topical analyses with CEOs of today's leading global companies. Visit mckinseyquarterly.com to watch the video interview or to read the full transcript.

of it is self-inflicted? And you've got to address the self-inflicted part as you get ready to come out.

The second is, determine how deep it's going to be and how long it's going to last and set your plan appropriately. It will usually be deeper and last longer than you think. The third one really ties back to getting closer to your customer at a point in time and using these downturns really to move into the market adjacencies. Combine discipline and process with innovation and willingness to try new things. Then, if it works, build the strategy around it. And that ties back to mistakes. We've made a lot of mistakes, but the ones that repeat are when we don't move fast enough. Almost all the windows of opportunities I've missed—areas that got ahead of us that we couldn't get back into without doing big acquisitions or something—have been when I've moved too slow. However, if you try to move too fast without a process behind it that can scale, have flexibility, and replicate—that's equally as bad as not moving fast at all.

The *Quarterly*: *You say you are going to be aggressive. What does that mean?*

John Chambers: We're seeing a large number of opportunities open up with tremendous speed, such as virtualization of the data center, where server technology and storage technology and network technology and software come together. If you don't move now, you get left behind. And this isn't about individual products, it's about how they play together architecturally to change business models.

We're fortunately structured in a way that we believe—and time will tell if we're right or wrong—allows us not to do one or two priorities, like we had done before, but almost three dozen. Productivity growth is all going to be around collaboration and the network-enabled technologies, called Web 2.0, that enable collaboration. And what you're seeing is a tremendous explosion in terms of the utilization of these technologies.

If you'd have told three or four years ago that I would eventually be blogging, I'd have said, "That's not going to happen." But blogging is now the way I communicate with our employees—almost all video. Our utilization of discussion forums is not up 160 percent over the last year, it's up 1,600 percent. Taking YouTube capabilities and bringing them internal—we call it CiscoVision—is up 3,100 percent, with 54,000 employees out of 66,000 using it in the last year. Use of Webex capabilities is up 3,900 percent.

Those are clearly numbers that indicate a new market transition. Investing in IT the last couple of years didn't necessarily get you the productivity or the standard of living change. It's these new technologies that will drive the next wave of productivity.

The *Quarterly*: *What does this mean for your customers? If I'm a company, tell me what this allows me to do and what the potential impact of these collaborations will be.*

John Chambers: Take, for example, when a customer walks into your store. You can identify who that customer is by a security camera. People often use those cameras not for security as much as for treating customers in a way the customer wants. If the associates and the management team recognize me when I go into a store and they know my buying patterns, they're able to help me more effectively. Say they know that I like fishing gear in Wal-Mart and they also know that I like Wal-Mart's deal on nice wines—they watch my buying behavior and then suddenly as I go past a digital sign, it could read, "We're having a special sale on fishing gear over here. And by the way, here's a wine that you may want to look at." That's going to come.

These new technologies can cut your travel budget with telepresence. Ours went from $750 million a year to $350 million a year, sustainable. And we've actually, under the economic challenges, dropped it to $240 million. So our average expenditure per employee has been probably 65 percent lower than what it was at the start and will not come back. All businesses will have this. It doesn't matter if you're a bank, a retailer, a manufacturer, or a high-tech company.

John Chambers

Vital statistics
Born August 23, 1949, in Cleveland, Ohio

Married, with 2 grown children

Education
Graduated with BS/BA (1971) in business and JD (1974) from West Virginia University

Earned MBA in finance and management in 1975 from Indiana University

Career highlights
Cisco Systems (1991–present)
• Chairman and CEO (2006–present)
• President and CEO (1995–present)
• Senior vice president, worldwide sales and operations (1991–95)

Wang Laboratories (1982–91)
• Vice president, US operations (1987–91)
• Fellow (1991–92)

IBM (1976–82)
• Technology sales

Fast facts
Named one of *Time*'s '100 Most Influential People' (2008); recipient of first-ever Clinton Global Citizen Award (2007) and Secretary of State's Award for Corporate Excellence (2005)

Earned Lifetime Achievement Award, Smithsonian Institute (2000); Distinguished Industry Leader Award, IEEE (2002); Most Powerful Person in Networking, *Network World* (2003)

The *Quarterly*: *How is Cisco reinventing and repositioning itself based on this new landscape?*

John Chambers: I always believe you deal with the world the way it is, not the way you wish it was. And what has changed is, our segment of the industry has moved from being "plumbers." And I'm proud to be a plumber. First, it's a very honorable profession. Second, you make a lot of money doing plumbing on the Internet.

But the future's about, how do you add intelligence to that plumbing? And how do you do it architecturally, from a technology point of view, so you can go from any device to any content over any combination of networks, data, voice, and video? Sounds simple, but it's really complex to do with security and predictability.

So we'll move from a company that sold plumbing—routers and technology—to a company that, if we do our job right, will be the most trusted business and technology adviser to the top companies in the world. That is the biggest transition. Now, the challenge is, you couldn't do that without different organization structures.

I'm a command-and-control guy. It clearly has worked well for me. I say, turn right, 66,600 people turn right. But that's not the future. The future's going to be all around collaboration and teamwork, with a structured process behind it. And that's the key. You can't move fast without a replicable process. So it's about speed, combined with technology enablement, combined with a replicable process.

The *Quarterly*: *Traditional management theory would say, "You have too many priorities. Pick a few; prioritize. How are you*

going to run a company without a straightforward organizational structure?" How do you respond to that?

John Chambers: Well, first, they could be right. Any time you take yourself too seriously and think that critics may not be right, you're already in trouble. However, we started modeling this in 2001. That's when we moved to social communities with a great deal of discipline. We created councils ($10 billion opportunities), boards ($1 billion opportunities), and working groups. Over the last eight years, we've done things right and we've made some mistakes, and we've adjusted—including the management team's skill sets and how they're rewarded.

We have a very disciplined vision five to ten years out of what we want to look like; what our true, sustainable differentiation is, which we've got to implement in two to four years; and then, execution-wise, what we're going to do the next 12 to 18 months. So we're able to play a portfolio with tremendous speed and efficiency. I might be involved in only two to three of the councils and boards and working groups. Each of our key executives does the same; and instead of 10 people running the company, with a very heavy leaning toward the command, we have a structure where the top 500 people run it today.

How companies are benefiting from Web 2.0:
Selected McKinsey Global Survey Results

Jacques Bughin

Web 2.0 technologies improve interactions with employees, customers, and suppliers at some companies more than at others. An outside study titled 'Power Law of Enterprise 2.0'[1] analyzed data from earlier McKinsey Web 2.0 surveys to better understand the factors that contribute most significantly to the successful use of these technologies.

The findings show that success follows a 'power curve distribution'—meaning, a small group of users accounts for the largest portion of the gains. According to our research, the 20 percent of users reporting the greatest satisfaction received 80 percent of the benefits. What's more, this 20 percent included 68 percent of the companies reporting the highest adoption rates for a range of Web 2.0 tools, 58 percent of the companies where use by employees was most widespread, and 82 percent of the respondents who claimed the highest levels of satisfaction from Web 2.0 use at their companies.

To better understand the underlying factors leading to these companies' success, we first created an index of Web 2.0 performance, combining the previously mentioned variables: adoption, breadth of employee use, and satisfaction. We then analyzed how these scores correlated with three company characteristics: the competitive environment (using industry type as a proxy), company features (the size and location of operations), and the extent to which the company actively managed Web 2.0. These three factors explained two-thirds of the companies' scores.

Also, while all of the factors are slightly correlated with one another—for example, there are more high-tech companies in the United States than in South America—each factor by itself explains much of why companies achieved their performance scores. Management capabilities ranked highest at 54 percent, meaning that good management is more than half of the battle in

Jacques Bughin is a director in McKinsey's Brussels office.

The *Quarterly*: *How does it actually work? Are these councils and boards empowered and do they make decisions?*

John Chambers: Well, they're empowered, but they have to know where they are. The classic question is, "Well, if I'm going to lead, don't I need to have people reporting to me and don't I need to control budget?" And the answer is, "No" and "No"—because that's not what cross-functional leadership is about. Cross-functional leadership is about doing a replicable process with a business model enabled by technology, and each functional groups being able to implement it.

Secondly, they've got to understand the implications of their decisions across all the functions. That was a learning curve for us, because we developed our people in silos. And third, you select who goes on these councils and boards by the leaders of the group, which originally were my executive VPs and senior VPs. So all of a sudden people try to be in every group. And it took about four councils and boards, and they couldn't keep up. So they had to delegate, they had to empower, they had to train. And it took us a while to change compensation and reward systems, but now it's a machine. You're talking about how we spend our time being dramatically changed. Theoretical eight years

ensuring satisfaction with Web 2.0, a high rate of adoption, and widespread use of the tools. The competitive environment explained 28 percent, size and location 17 percent.

Parsing these results even further, we found that three aspects of management were particularly critical to superior performance: a lack of internal barriers to Web 2.0, a culture favoring open collaboration (a factor confirmed in the 2009 survey), and early adoption of Web 2.0 technologies. The high-tech and telecommunications industries had higher scores than manufacturing, while companies with sales of less than $1 billion or those located in the United States were more likely to have relatively high performance scores than larger companies located elsewhere.

While the evidence suggests that focused management improves Web 2.0 performance, there's still a way to go before users become as satisfied with these technologies as they are with others. The top 20 percent of companies reached a performance score of only 35 percent (the score increased to 44 percent in the 2009 survey). When the same score methodology is applied to technologies that corporations had previously adopted, Web 2.0's score is below the 57 percent for traditional corporate IT services, such as e-mail, and the 80 percent for mobile-communications services.

[1] See Yin Lee, ed., *Encyclopedia of E-Business Development and Management in the Digital Economy* (IGI Global, forthcoming 2009).

The full results of this survey, 'How companies are benefiting from Web 2.0: McKinsey Global Survey Results,' are available on mckinseyquarterly.com/surveys.

ago; started to work about four years ago; replicated with tremendous speed today.

The *Quarterly*: *Do you think this is a model that most other companies can replicate?*

John Chambers: I think it is actually much more replicable than the command-and-control, top-down approach I did before. The top-down model was based upon really growing up within the company, being a part of taking it from $70 million to about $35 billion, being able to watch one product grow to two, being through five economic downturns, developing the game book for our approaches.

That is command and control, and it is tremendously dependant upon your top leaders. What we have now is an organizational structure that I think is built for the future. It's designed to answer the question, "How do you leverage the power of the human network to really move on decisions and directions?" Sounds like nice marketing, but I think five years from now this will be the future of business models.

The *Quarterly*: *As you think about your role as leader, what do you find to be the limiting factor?*

John Chambers: I'm the roadblock. In command and control, the enabler is the CEO. Where the industry's going though, in every industry, will be about how you change. How do you get outside your comfort zone? How do you basically catch your marks, transitions, and move on? Let's use the current economic downturn. When you have an economic downturn of this challenge, 20 to 40 percent of the companies will never get back to where they were before. Never.

Related articles on mckinseyquarterly.com

High tech: Finding opportunity in the downturn

Google's view on the future of business: An interview with CEO Eric Schmidt

Hal Varian on how the Web challenges managers

And the key is, how do you focus that opportunity in a way that not only allows you to return to where you were before but to continue to grow? And so, part of it is the ability to paint a picture of what's possible. Part of it is also to manage inside our own minds and our hearts a combination of opportunity and the sense that if you don't move, you will get left behind.

The *Quarterly*: *How do you motivate your employees?*

John Chambers: If they aren't excited about the vision, they probably aren't here any more. But you do sell to your employees, and you've got to communicate, communicate, communicate. You need to do the same with your customers and shareholders in a very transparent fashion.

You show what's possible, why you're doing this, what milestones they ought to watch.

It's having the courage, as leadership, to change. And often the best leaders are the most resistant to change. About 20 percent of my leaders didn't make the transition. They were command-and-control, wonderful leaders but wanted to stay command and control and couldn't transition over. And I had nothing against that. It's like a basketball player who can score 30 points a game. But if you're going to go into a real, unique style of team offense and team defense, if a person can't adjust then it's probably better to trade him to another team. So all of us have to change. And the leader has to not only say the talk, she or he has got to walk the talk. Got to be the best example.

The *Quarterly*: *How do you change personally?*

John Chambers: One thing has not changed about Cisco in the almost 19 years I've been here is that we are driven by our customers. Customers tell you about transitions, and you must then drive it down through the organization. To do that, I have to change the organization structure. I have to change my style. I have to listen differently. I attend telepresence sessions where industry analysts from 12 different locations are in the same room. I listen to what they think we're doing well—and, most importantly, to what we have to do differently.

If you plant a thousand seeds and let a thousand seeds bloom, you get a weed field. It isn't just about speed or innovation. It's about operational excellence, combined with the capability to scale and to replicate. So I had to change. And I had to realize that I would either be part of the future success, or I would be the one that would slow us down. And you've got to get people around you—customers and twenty somethings—that really challenge you. Especially during major, violent economic or market disruptions, you've got to move fast. And you've got to be willing to listen and try new things.

Copyright © 2009
McKinsey & Company.
All rights reserved.

We welcome your comments on this article. Please send them to quarterly_comments@ mckinsey.com.

If you think that you cannot be left behind, you're wrong—regardless of what position you're in. If you adopt the philosophy of "I have no choice; I've just got to hunker down and survive," your survival rate goes down dramatically, and you will probably miss the biggest opportunity of your business career on what's occurring now. So it's the balancing. It's not an "or," it's an "and." How do you do innovation and execution? How do you behave financially conservatively during the toughest economic challenge we've seen in our lifetime, yet use this challenge in a way that repositions you for the future? And then, how do you use technology in ways that you've probably not thought of—that are easy to use, video based, network enabled—to change your business process and to change what you do for society? Sounds high level, but it's remarkably effective. o

Bill Butcher

Special report

China + US: Collaborating on clean energy

China
+ US

As December's climate change conference in Copenhagen approaches, all eyes are on China and the United States to see what sort of partnership will develop. The opportunity for clean-energy technology is within reach, but only if these two countries can collaborate to set a feasible agenda.

These articles explore the challenges and the potential behind a China–US partnership and examine the technologies currently available and how they can be successfully implemented.

China and the US:
The potential of a clean-tech partnership

Only a collaboration between the world's two largest carbon emitters will create an environment where clean-energy technologies can thrive.

Jonathan Woetzel

Jonathan Woetzel is a director in McKinsey's Shanghai office.

China and the United States, the world's dominant producers of carbon emissions, have adopted aggressive programs to reduce oil imports, create new clean-energy industries and jobs, and generally improve the environment. But the environment that will be most critical to making or breaking the two countries' efforts to curb the dangers of global warming could well be the market that they jointly create in pursuit of their aims. Unless the two work together to provide the scale, standards, and technology transfer necessary to make a handful of promising but expensive new clean-energy technologies successful, momentum to curb global warming could stall and neither country will maximize its gains in terms of green jobs, new companies, and energy security.

The risk is real. Electrified vehicles, carbon capture and storage (CCS), and concentrated solar power, among other emerging "green tech" sectors, will need massive investment, infrastructure, and research to get off the ground. While the Chinese and US governments, along with private investors, are pursuing all of these technologies, they cannot achieve separately what they could jointly.

Whether collaborating formally or informally, China and the United States working as a group of two (or G-2) dedicated to controlling climate change would boost these technologies and deliver benefits that would accrue to all nations. Clean-energy solutions are critical for reducing the amount of harmful greenhouse gases produced not only by the two highest-emitting nations but also by countries worldwide. For instance, if the majority of vehicles on the world's roads by 2030 were hybrids and battery-powered vehicles, they would generate 42 percent fewer emissions than if all cars continued to run on today's gas and diesel engines.[1] But such reductions won't occur—won't even come close to happening—unless China and the United States lay the groundwork to make it so.

A global electric-car sector must start in China and the United States, and it must begin with the two countries jointly creating an environment for automotive investors to scale their bets across both nations. Private companies in China and the United States will most certainly compete to make the products, including electric-drive (or hybrid) vehicles, batteries, charging stations, and so on. But the two governments can no doubt create the conditions for both of them to succeed— for example, by setting coordinated product and safety standards across the two markets, funding the rollout of infrastructure, sponsoring joint R&D initiatives in select areas (such as new materials for car parts), ensuring that trade policies support rather than hinder the development of a global supply chain for the sector, and providing consumers with financial incentives to buy the new models. More immediately, the two governments could pick matching cities in China and the United States for electrified-vehicle pilots that could be used to collect standardized data on real electrified-vehicle consumer adoption, infrastructure costs, and driving conditions that could then be shared with companies in both nations.

This new sector will require scale to succeed—more scale than could be found any time soon in either country alone. Electrified vehicles may one day become a viable market within both nations, but that day will arrive much more quickly if the two countries collaborate to create a market that is bigger and more attractive. In building this market, China and the United States would also ensure that the companies and jobs associated with it would be created in both countries sooner. Oil consumption will fall more quickly as well: today, about 50 percent of China's oil imports—and 80 percent of America's— are used to fuel vehicles. In other words, one plus one would equal

[1] For more information, see the full report, *Pathways to a Low-Carbon Economy: Version 2 of the Global Greenhouse Gas Abatement Cost Curve*, McKinsey & Company, January 2009. Emissions abatement could be even higher if the electricity used to recharge car batteries is clean.

three. Such momentum would also likely spark Europe into competing in a global electrified-vehicle industry faster.

CCS is another technology whose success needs the scale that only China and the United States can create together. Adapting CCS technology to coal-fired plants to capture the emitted greenhouse gases is expensive. CCS technology also uses a lot of energy to capture the emissions, thereby making plants less efficient. And fundamental questions about how the captured emissions are to be stored still need addressing. Neither nation is pursuing this expensive, uncertain emissions reduction technology quickly, but both would improve their chances and their options if they pooled costs and knowledge.

Together, the two governments could fund demonstration plants in China and the United States, jointly evaluate technologies available from vendors, set standards, and drive down costs. By using the pilot plants as research labs to learn more about the challenges CCS faces and how to overcome them, the governments could share the information with companies entering the CCS business, advancing learning in this industry at a quicker pace. Assuming engineers find solutions to the technical and storage hurdles, we estimate that by 2030 this technology could "clean" 17 percent of coal power in the United States and 30 percent of China's coal power, reducing total combined emissions by as much as 7 percent—a significant benefit to both nations and the rest of the world.

Concentrated solar power (CSP) might not even have a future without joint action by China and the United States. As an emerging technology, CSP requires both technical progress and massive investments that only the largest economies can support. CSP technology uses sunlight to create and store steam power to drive turbines that can transmit electricity on a larger scale more easily than they could using photo-voltaic technology (which uses flat-screen receptors that turn sunlight into power). If clean concentrated solar power is scaled to generate 22 percent of total power in China and the United States by 2030, it could create over half a million jobs in each country. Setting common standards, coinvesting in pilot projects and R&D, and undertaking other joint initiatives are the way to get this started.

There are other benefits to joint action on clean energy besides reducing oil imports, cleaning up the air, and creating jobs. Cooperation on tangible actions that result in positive improvements for each country could help to foster trust between governments that have real differences on other political and economic issues. In addition, meaningful reductions in oil consumption by the world's two largest importers of oil could ease pressure on future imbalances of global supply and demand of the fossil fuel.

It won't be easy for countries and companies to work in common to make these technologies real. The challenges to cooperation are numerous. Companies in both nations will be wary about what information they share with partners and competitors. Real cooperation between the two countries on technology initiatives is limited, so both sides will have to work hard to build relationships. In addition, they will need to create institutional frameworks for implementing and managing projects, as well as cofinancing mechanisms, partnership rules, and governance models. US companies will be concerned about protecting the intellectual property (IP) technologies that they use in pilot projects in China. The two governments will need to cleanly separate bilateral initiatives on clean-energy development from broader, multilateral agreements on emissions reductions. The list goes on.

But none of these challenges are showstoppers. Negotiations between the two countries could address nearly all these issues comprehensively. Even the thorniest—IP protection—is manageable. Because companies from many nations would contribute to making these three big technologies a success, IP agreements should be international. On that front, China will need to improve its ability to enforce global IP rules. Most critical, however, is the leadership that will be needed to surmount these obstacles. A commitment at the top levels of both governments to set a joint course for making these technologies real would be the signal of a true beginning. From there, the impulse for collaboration may well filter down through the public and private sectors in the two countries to make research, investment, and policy a cooperative agenda.○

Related articles on mckinseyquarterly.com

China's green opportunity

Cleaner energy for China: An interview with the chairman of ENN Group

What China can learn from Japan on cleaning up the environment

Copyright © 2009 McKinsey & Company. All rights reserved.

We welcome your comments on this article. Please send them to quarterly_comments@ mckinsey.com.

Opportunities in three clean-energy technologies

China and the United States are the world's largest energy users, importers, and polluters. By collaborating on high-impact clean-energy technologies, the two countries can create markets at a scale required for success.

The following pages offer a closer look at the results possible by 2030 and what it will take to achieve to achieve them.

For an interactive presentation on this topic, see 'China and the US: The potential of a clean-tech partnership,' on mckinseyquarterly.com.

Electrified vehicles

If penetration of electrified vehicles (EVs) rises above 45 percent in China and the United States by 2030, oil imports and CO_2 emissions would fall dramatically.

	By 2030	Results		
China	**40 million** EVs **0.7 million** charging stations	**62%** of new auto sales	**16%** oil import reduction	**0.4-gigaton** annual CO_2 emission reduction relative to internal-combustion engine
United States	**70 million** EVs **1.2 million** charging stations	**46%** of new auto sales	**18%** oil import reduction	**0.7-gigaton** annual CO_2 emission reduction relative to internal-combustion engine

Concentrated solar power

By 2030, concentrated solar power (CSP) could supply about 22 percent of the electricity in China and the United States.

	By 2030	Results		
China	**100-gigawatt** installed base **7,000 square miles** of land	**22%** of total electricity supplied	**1.7-gigaton** annual CO_2 emission reduction	**500,000+ jobs** created
United States	**75-gigawatt** installed base **4,600 square miles** of land	**22%** of total electricity supplied	**1.1-gigaton** annual CO_2 emission reduction	**500,000+ jobs** created

Carbon capture and storage

By 2030, efficient carbon capture and storage (CCS) technology could be ready for large-scale implementation.

	By 2030	Results	
China	**410-gigawatt** installed capacity **35%** of electrical supply	**30%** of coal capacity scrubbed	**1.5-gigaton** annual CO_2 emission reduction
United States	**60-gigawatt** installed capacity **4%** of electrical supply	**17%** of coal capacity scrubbed	**0.3-gigaton** annual CO_2 emission reduction

Achieving an adoption rate of more than 45 percent for EVs by 2030 would require significant investment and technology development, mass production capacity, and an installed infrastructure.

Investment	Key drivers for adoption
$28 billion	Battery technology breakthrough by 2012–16
	Future oil prices influence operating economies of EVs
	Policies that encourage consumers to purchase EVs
$50 billion	Infrastructure buildout in China and the United States

CSP's high capital cost will require larger annual investments to 2030, as well as near-term subsidies to help it compete with fossil fuels.

Annual investment	Key drivers for adoption
$24 billion	Land must have a lot of direct sunlight and provide access to water
	Current technology cannot compete against fossil fuels without subsidy
	Intellectual property must be shared between China and the United States
$16 billion	Transmission grid must be improved to carry electricity from plants to cities

CCS will require incremental investments and subsidies to achieve results by 2030. Currently, plants with CCS represent a 60 percent capital cost premium over those without it.

Investment	Assumptions for investment
$11 billion	20% of all new coal capacity will use CCS by 2020
	100% of plants will use CCS after 2030
$2.7 billion	40% of all new US coal capacity will use CCS by 2020
	After 2025, no new coal plants will be created, as fuel mix shifts to renewables

Setting the global climate agenda:

An interview with Kenneth Lieberthal

Thomas J. Kiely

In December 2009, representatives from nearly 200 nations will gather in Copenhagen to negotiate a global agreement for reducing greenhouse gas emissions. As the meeting draws near, much of the international community is looking to China and the United States—the world's biggest carbon emitters—to help set the agenda for global climate efforts.

In this interview, foreign-policy expert Kenneth Lieberthal sketches out the path toward Copenhagen and the difficult questions both China and the United States must address in the coming months. Lieberthal, a visiting fellow at the Brookings Institution and an expert on energy policy and China–US relations, explains the scope of the opportunities that cooperation on clean-energy development could create, the remaining roadblocks to compromise, and his hunch that a clean-energy partnership between the two countries will emerge before December.

Tom Kiely, a member of *McKinsey Quarterly's* board of editors, spoke with Lieberthal in June 2009 at the Brookings Institution, in Washington, DC. What follows is an excerpt from the full interview, 'How China and the US will set the global climate agenda,' available on mckinseyquarterly.com.

The Quarterly: *How would an agreement between China and the United States on clean-energy development affect global discussions on climate change at the UN meeting in Copenhagen?*

Kenneth Lieberthal: If the US and China can demonstrate that we are prepared to do a lot on our own—and to do a lot together—to address this issue, it increases, tremendously, the momentum going into Copenhagen. I don't think Copenhagen will necessarily get to a final agreement on a new framework. I'm hoping it at least reaches an agreement on the *shape*

of an agreement for a new framework and then fills in the details in the year or so after that.

The chances of leading to a good final agreement are much better if the US and China demonstrate that they are serious and able to cooperate—bringing together the biggest industrialized country and the biggest developing country to address a common issue that has divided industrialized and developing countries on matters of principle until now.

What we're hoping to get is a US–China clean-energy partnership, as a formal agreement. If everything goes well, I would expect it to be signed when the two presidents [Barack Obama and Hu Jintao] meet late this year.

The Quarterly: *Where does cooperation on this topic fit within the broader context of China–US relations?*

Kenneth Lieberthal: This is basically a new issue and it has rapidly moved to the center of the relationship. I would argue it's one of the two or three most important issues that are going to shape this relationship. If we can reach an agreement on a partnership here and fill that with real content, this is the kind of issue that involves cooperation that goes well beyond the security realm and the foreign-policy specialists.

Energy gets to the core of each economy and involves an array of people who normally don't deal with each other. And this is an issue that is not going to go away in two or three years. So if we can build a whole framework for cooperation, it will probably, over a period of years, have a profoundly positive effect on US–China relations—expanding the relationship, deepening it, and, over time, reducing the mistrust that currently still exists.

Tom Kiely is a member of *McKinsey Quarterly's* board of editors.

Watch the full video interview with Kenneth Lieberthal on mckinseyquarterly.com.

The *Quarterly*: *Is there a downside risk to relations if clean-energy cooperation doesn't work as planned?*

Kenneth Lieberthal: Yes. If we try to engage on this and find we really cannot see eye to eye enough to cooperate on it, it will become a major additional source of tension and of distrust in our relationship, not that anyone wants that to happen. But when you're dealing with an issue as profound as where the world is headed—in terms of capacity to deal with a global threat such as climate change—and you can't reach a basic level of understanding with the other major player, that does not contribute to a perception of mutual confidence and an ability to work together in the future.

The biggest failure is that each side has serious doubts about the long-term intentions of the other side of this relationship. It is hard to find a high-level official or an intellectual in China who doesn't believe that sooner or later the US will try to slow down or stop China's rise. The assumption there is that the US is too zero-sum in its thinking to sit back contentedly as China becomes stronger and stronger and, in a sense, reduces US global dominance. In the US, there is a concern that if China reaches its full potential, it has on its agenda to marginalize the US and Asia. Each side doubts the intentions of the other, and when you doubt them, you hedge. You look at the other guy's hedge and you say, 'See, my doubts were justified,' and you can get a self-fulfilling prophecy. So I think that these big global issues now actually provide the best opportunity to begin to build confidence.

The *Quarterly*: *Can the framework for multilateral discussions at Copenhagen help manage the risk?*

Kenneth Lieberthal: As we talk about a US–China clean-energy partnership and the multilateral negotiations for Copenhagen, it's important for us to keep those distinct. When the Chinese deal with Copenhagen, they also have to be concerned about the Group of 77[1] and the other foreign-policy issues that can complicate the negotiation of a clean-energy partnership.

If we get the clean-energy partnership, it will have a positive spillover effect with Copenhagen. If we let the two discussions get commingled, then I'm afraid it's going to make it much more difficult to get to the clean-energy partnership, and therefore we might lose the upside for Copenhagen too. So there's a subtle but very important management problem in these two streams of negotiations, in part because many of the same people participate in both streams.

Face it, any objective analysis of what has to be done to get ahead of the curve in dealing with climate change has to leave you very, very worried. But if you look at the capacity to begin to work seriously on this issue, I think one has to be quite optimistic. This has really shifted very, very rapidly recently. I think that the momentum is now shifting in the direction of getting a deal done.

[1] The Group of 77, or G-77, is a UN organization of 77 developing countries.

© Floriane de Lassée, *Moscow series*, 2008
Courtesy CM ART

How Russia could be more productive

The way out of the economic slowdown is
a more effective use of the country's resources—
not just *more* resources.

Vitaly Klintsov, Irene Shvakman, and Yermolai Solzhenitsyn

Russia's economy, like the world economy as a whole, fell off a cliff during the first half of 2009, with GDP down roughly 10 percent.[1] It's a movie the country has seen before: GDP fell more than 40 percent following the Soviet Union's collapse, in 1991, and in 1998 Russia defaulted on its debt, the ruble plummeted, and economy-wide capacity utilization fell below 50 percent.

Last time around, Russia experienced a dramatic economic turnaround: GDP grew at an average annual rate of 7 percent between 1998 and 2007, vaulting the country to 53rd (from 72nd) in the world rankings of wealth. Wages increased strongly as well, with disposable income rising 26 percent a year in nominal terms.

Pulling off a similar rebound will be more challenging now. Even before the global downturn, capacity utilization was approaching 80 percent, and the days of relatively easy expansion through better use of the existing capital stock were drawing to a close. An increase in the size of Russia's workforce, which accounted for almost one-third of the growth in real per capita GDP over the past decade (exhibit), was going into reverse. In fact, Russia's labor force could shrink by as many as ten million people by 2020. The financial crisis has made raising

Vitaly Klintsov is a principal in McKinsey's Moscow office, where **Irene Shvakman** and **Yermolai Solzhenitsyn** are directors.

[1] On July 15, 2009, the economic-development minister, Elvira Nabiullina, estimated that Russia's gross domestic product contracted by 10.1 percent in the first half of 2009, compared with the same period in 2008.

Exhibit: **On the fast track**

Russia's economy has been growing rapidly over the past decade.

Russia's per capita GDP growth[1]

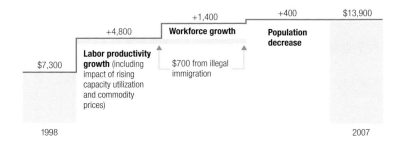

[1] At purchasing-power parity; 2005 real dollars.

Source: Global Insight; Ministry for Economic Development of the Russian Federation; McKinsey analysis

capital for investments more difficult and has battered commodity prices—including those of oil, metal ores, and coal. Commodities collectively represented around 20 percent of Russia's GDP in recent years. Now Russia must grow by making better use of labor and capital resources—in short, higher productivity. The McKinsey Global Institute (MGI) has twice studied Russian labor productivity: first in 1999 and now in 2009.[2] During the intervening years, economy-wide labor productivity increased to 31 percent of US levels, from 22 percent.

To make another leap in productivity and economic performance, Russia must tackle deep structural challenges, such as boosting its competitive intensity, making nuts-and-bolts improvements in operations and business processes, simplifying and clarifying regulations (including those for urban planning and permissions), and allocating financial capital more efficiently. There's also a human dimension: raising productivity will require a more skilled and mobile workforce.

But Russia has some advantages. It can grow robustly without the need for rapid urbanization and social transformation—needs that are so acute in other emerging markets, notably China and India, countries whose productivity lags behind Russia's significantly. And there's a silver lining to Russia's massive investment requirements: as demand for capital outstrips domestic supply, competition for foreign funds will probably make it necessary to speed up the implementation of Russia's productivity agenda. Finally, the country's government, which must play a critical role, has a powerful incentive to move quickly.

[2] For a synopsis of the 1999 report, see Alexei Beltyukov, M. James Kondo, William W. Lewis, Michael M. Obermayer, Vincent Palmade, and Alex Reznikovitch, "Reflections on Russia," mckinseyquarterly.com, February 2000. For the full MGI report, see *Unlocking Economic Growth in Russia*, available free of charge online at mckinsey.com/mgi.

In recent years, oil-related taxes represented a third to half of federal revenues. If these receipts shrink, Russia will need new ones. Broad-based, productivity-led growth, while far from easy to realize, is an achievable way to create new revenue sources while improving the lives of Russia's people.

A sector-based view

Our research is grounded in an analysis of five important sectors: electric power, retailing, steel, residential construction, and retail banking. Their labor productivity now ranges from 15 percent of US levels, in electric power, to 33 percent, in steel.

Three shortcomings are common to all of these sectors: inefficient business processes, obsolete capacity and production methods, and structural problems attributable to economy-wide factors, such

Insider perspective: Analyzing the bottlenecks

Vladislav Baumgertner
President and general director of the potassium fertilizer producer Urlakali

We've been working to improve productivity for nearly two years, and my experience is that the major constraints are internal.

The biggest scope for productivity improvement is in our business processes, which are redundant, and in the level of automation, which is pretty low. Some time ago, we did some benchmarking research in the potassium industry and saw that the productivity of labor in Russia is about nine or ten times below that of our foreign competitors. We also looked at logistics, procurement, quality management, and so on. In all of these areas, productivity was several times below that of our foreign competition.

'We sometimes find up to nine or ten management levels between the blue-collar worker and the director general'

Naturally, one of the main reasons for this is that the standards and technical specifications employed in the construction of our plants are from many decades ago. We also inherited a culture that resists delegating tasks, with

a lot of management layers between the general director and the people actually on the ground. In our case, we sometimes find up to nine or ten management levels between the blue-collar worker and the director general.

The next constraint is that, 'genetically,' we are used to increasing production by, let's say, digging an additional mine or buying an extra machine tool—rather than by producing more in the same plant after analyzing bottlenecks. Another vast problem is a lack of motivation. Everything starts from that. Motivation should be present at the top and it should be transferred internally to all management levels and to all blue-collar workers.

Really increasing productivity consists not in making one or two radical decisions. It involves a long-term process of making hundreds of small-scale decisions that change the corporate culture, the motivation, and the mentality of people who work on the floor level. Making these changes should be on the agenda of senior management.

as income levels that are lower than those prevailing in advanced economies. Depending on the sector, inefficient processes account for 30 to 80 percent of the labor productivity gap with the United States, outdated capacity for 20 to 60 percent, and structural factors for 5 to 15 percent. (For a view of the barriers to productivity from the general director of a Russian potassium fertilizer producer, see the sidebar "Insider perspective: Analyzing the bottlenecks.")

The underlying causes of these shortcomings are diverse. Differing levels of competition within sectors clearly play a role: retailing and steel are the most productive and competitive of the five sectors we studied, while electric power and construction are among the least on both fronts. Regulatory procedures and processes may obstruct operational improvements. Complex, opaque rules for planning and permissions make development projects riskier, and the absence of a comprehensive financial infrastructure hampers the efficient raising and allocation of capital. These challenges cut across each sector we studied, but to make them—and the potential solutions—more tangible, we address them in the context of individual economic sectors.

Russia's electric-power sector is the world's fourth largest, but it suffers from aging assets and labor productivity that is just 15 percent of the US level.

© Nikita Kryuchkov/ITAR-TASS
Leningrad region, Russia

The competition problem in electric power

Russia's electric-power sector, a monopoly until 2008, is a poster child for the inefficiencies arising in the absence of vigorous competition. Although the sector is the world's fourth largest, its labor productivity is just 15 percent of the US level. The end, last year, of the electric-power monopoly could stimulate productivity growth, but only if real market-based price competition emerges. (For a view of the electric-power sector from leaders of an established Russian player and a new entrant from Italy, see the sidebar "Insider perspective: Change and transformation.")

The industry's central challenge is that Russia must replace much of its aging capacity, but electricity prices don't cover the full cost of investments in new plants. Without price liberalization, private power companies have little reason to invest in new generating capacity— and the government has historically favored low prices as a social good.

One way the government could help make plants cheaper to build (and perhaps limit the price increases needed to pay for them) would be to relax complex equipment-licensing procedures. These rules—combined with the sector's suboptimal procurement practices, opaque cost controls, and lack of standardization—make building new capacity pricier than it is in other countries. Coal-fired plants, for example, are 25 to 40 percent more expensive than similar facilities in Europe and the United States.

Insider perspective: Change and transformation

Vitaly Yakovlev
General director of the electric-power company Mosenergo

We are quite an old company, with old electric stations. Companies created before 1991 differ a great deal from those created afterward. Old companies have an authoritarian style of management, midlevel managers who lack initiative and are reluctant to change business processes, low levels of automation, and other inherent aspects of the old economy.

'Technical upgrades of electric-power stations are very hard, and changing business processes is a challenge'

But the entire system works in harmony, and those companies don't have problems until the new economic order exposes them to a new level of competition. Even then, the personnel and management are reluctant to change; technical upgrades of electric-power stations are very hard, and changing business processes is a challenge.

So we need a full-fledged program of change and transformation—not surgical operations on the infrastructure or business processes. It should be applicable to all aspects of the company, including the culture and the entire management structure, which needs to be more flat, so that lower-level personnel get more responsibility for decision making.

Carlo Tamburi
Head of the international division of the Italian energy company Enel

It was only a year ago that OGK-5 joined the Enel Group, so the process has just started. But this comes after we had a couple of very good success stories in Slovakia and Bulgaria, which from both a technological and a cultural point of view are comparable to Russia. In Bulgaria, we had a coal-fired plant that was very inefficient. We streamlined the organization, 'rightsizing' the personnel in agreement with the unions, from 1,100 people to 450 in five years, without suffering any problems, while increasing available generating capacity by almost 10 percent. We've experienced similar ratios in Slovakia, where on the nuclear side our key metrics are now in line with those of best-in-class players.

So that's what we are expecting from the Russian plants. We have four plants—one coal and the other three natural gas. These plants basically were run as four individual companies, with a lot of local power vested in the plant directors. We have changed some processes, like procurement and IT systems. We have centralized and rationalized them. People are quite receptive. And we have found a lot of technical competencies, a lot of technical skills. Actually, we want to leverage local skills and competencies, and we hire local guys with an international mind-set.

The sector itself can do much to boost the efficiency of existing operations. Russia's coal-fired plants are 8 percent less fuel efficient
than European ones, and its gas-powered plants are 6 percent less
fuel efficient. The low density and long distances of Russia's high-
voltage transmission lines raise technical "leakages" to almost twice
the US level. Commercial transmission losses are four times higher
because of electricity "theft"—the nonpayment of bills and inaccu-
rate metering. Tackling these problems will make a difference.
Nonetheless, productivity won't leap ahead until competitive pricing
gives the sector financial incentives to replace obsolete generating
capacity and to reduce operating costs in existing plants.

The road to operational excellence in retailing and steel
Competition isn't the problem for Russia's retailing and steel
sectors: both have no government-owned enterprises, and retailers
face foreign rivals at home, while the steelmakers contend with

Insider perspective: Too many signatures

Helmut Wieser
Executive vice president of the aluminum producer Alcoa and group president of its global rolled-products unit

We run 350 operations in over 30 countries.
When you have so many plants, you need
a sustainable business process, stable results,
continuity, and clear targets and monitoring.
So we adapted the Toyota production concept
and refined it given our specific circumstances, industry focus, and company culture.
We call this the Alcoa business system.

*'From a productivity perspective, here
in Russia we have too many people in
administrative units, support units,
and in the capital authorization structure'*

To engage the workforce and to change mind-
sets is a big task. At Samara Metallurgical Plant,
for example, we have over 4,000 employees.
It's the largest rolling facility in Europe and our
biggest plant in the whole Alcoa system. I go
around four times a year to the plants and work
there on the shop floor. I have a supervisor.
If you go to the plant and you work, you learn
what's really going on.

Last year in Russia, we had a production run of
seven days. Today we produce the same amount
of output in three days. We're seeing significant
step changes, and this has always been my experience in manufacturing. The reality for me is
that there's no difference if I work at an Alcoa plant
in China, Russia, Tennessee, Indiana, or Iowa.
You energize people, motivate, lead by example,
show what can be achieved.

From a productivity perspective, here in Russia
we have too many people in administrative units,
support units, and in the capital authorization
structure. As an example, we needed 16 signatures to get capital authorization at the plants in
2005. If you need 16 signatures to get $500,000
approved, it doesn't work. Your project is
delayed; you lose productivity every second. So we
had to move fast to change that in the business
process. We also put in new IT systems, which
always cost more in the beginning but are abso-
lutely necessary for long-term sustainable results.
We have an 'e-request' for electronic authorization that goes practically in one day now. These
are big changes.

Russian retail has transformed over the past decade. Seven million Russians work in the sector, turnover is six times higher than it was, and productivity has doubled.

© Gideon Mendel/ Corbis
Irkutsk, Russia

global competitors in Russia's export markets. But although these are the most productive sectors we studied, both still have huge opportunities—for the steelmakers, shutting down antiquated technology; for the retailers, replacing dated store formats and improving business processes.

Such opportunities exist, in part because of complicated, time-consuming regulatory procedures and processes. These slow down not only the development of commercial real estate (and therefore the modernization of retail formats) but also the consolidation of the steel sector and the adoption of lean business processes. (For executive views on business process improvements in another metal industry, aluminum, see the sidebar "Insider perspective: Too many signatures.")

Retailing. Over the past decade, Russian retailing (which, with the whole-sale sector, accounts for 10 percent of GDP) has increased its turnover sixfold, created five million new jobs, and doubled its productivity from 15 percent of the US level to 31 percent today—the best performance of the five sectors we analyzed. The heart of this transformation was the rise of modern retail formats, which are three times as productive as traditional ones.

Despite this progress, modern formats account for just 11 percent of retail employment and 35 percent of sales in Russia, compared with 82 and 86 percent of retail turnover in France and Germany, respectively. To double the retailing sector's productivity, Russia must increase the share of modern formats dramatically. In fact, the country should also boost their productivity, which lags behind that of their counterparts elsewhere. Russia's modern outlets, for instance, employ nearly three times as many people per square meter of retail space as their US counterparts do, and their workforce isn't well organized; staffing levels, for example, are often out of synch with customer traffic. But the throngs of customers who fill Russia's modern-format stores help compensate for their higher operating costs: revenues per square meter are roughly two times those in the United States.

Overall, the low share of modern formats in Russian retailing accounts for three-quarters of the productivity gap with the United States; the rest is due to inefficient processes. The country's network of roads is congested and underdeveloped, lengthening delivery times and increasing transport costs. The domination of logistics networks by small regional providers means that supply chains tend to be fragmented and therefore unreliable. Russian stores also don't exploit IT sufficiently and use part-time labor much less than their counterparts in other markets do, so they are overstaffed during low-traffic periods and understaffed during peak ones.

Upgrading these operating practices represents an enormous opportunity for Russian retailers, which should start now to centralize their administrative functions, optimize staffing, and improve processes. The current economic squeeze also gives retailers an opportunity to acquire new sites at lower prices and to consolidate smaller and poorly performing players. The government can help by streamlining regulations in order to accelerate the construction of new commercial real-estate projects, which are often dramatically more expensive than they are in developed countries, and by improving the transport and utility infrastructure.

Steel. Russia has traditionally had a strong, globally competitive steel industry, which accounts for 3 percent of the country's GDP and 6 percent of its exports and employs more than a million people. The industry's productivity has risen sharply since 1997, but almost entirely on the back of higher capacity utilization, not improved efficiency.

Outdated, subscale steelmaking technology is a major cause of the industry's low productivity in Russia: it still produces 16 percent of its steel in open-hearth rather than basic oxygen furnaces, which are 50 percent more labor efficient. The other reason for the low produc-

Russian steel has traditionally been globally competitive. But tougher market conditions on the horizon will make higher productivity a priority.

© Gerd Ludwig/Corbis
Novokuznetsk, Russia

tivity is inefficient business processes. Russian steelmakers employ 60 to 100 percent more administrative workers than best-practice companies do.

Higher productivity is achievable—already, the top three plants in Russia operate at 77 percent of US levels, more than three times the productivity of the country's smaller, older plants. Significant opportunities remain to boost the industry's productivity through automation, IT investments, and improved work organization. The government can lend support by emulating the European Union's approach to rationalizing its steel industry: job creation, retraining, and outsourcing and subcontracting programs.

The planning and permissions imperatives in residential construction

A lack of effective planning increases the uncertainty and risks of development projects in every sector we studied. But its impact is particularly pronounced in residential construction, which accounts for 6 percent of Russia's GDP and 8 percent of official employment. Just before the crisis, Russia's government committed itself to increasing per capita housing space to 33 square meters, from 21, by 2020, in line with EU levels. This standard would require average yearly residential construction at more than twice its historic peak. Improving the sector's productivity—now 21 percent of the US level—is vital to spur the supply of new housing.

It takes, on average, 700 days to get a construction permit in Russia—significantly longer than in Brazil, China, and India, and six times longer than in Sweden. Extended project cycles make planning less effective and create supply chain and financing problems; bank financing is virtually unobtainable for small and medium-sized devel-

Just before the global financial crisis, Russia committed itself to increasing per capita housing to double its historical level. Achieving this aim amid difficult economic conditions will require a step change in productivity.

© Arctic-Images/Corbis
Kanchalan, Chukot Autonomous District, Russia

opers. The risk and uncertainty for both them and investors is all the greater because two-thirds of Russia's cities haven't approved the master plans required by the country's city building codes. Developing and ensuring the effective implementation of such plans for cities and regions, along with creating a unified database of land plots, would make construction more productive by minimizing the time required to obtain permits and approvals. When Russia took such steps for construction projects related to the 2014 Winter Olympics in Sochi, approval times fell to six months, from three years.

Regulatory issues aren't the only problems bedeviling Russian residential construction. The industry, for example, should increase its use of productive modern materials and build larger housing developments. Only 17 percent of Russia's new houses, compared with 70 to 80 percent of US ones, take advantage of high-productivity prefabricated wall materials (including concrete and wooden panels) and metal frames. Similarly, traditional homes built, with relatively unproductive methods, by their future occupants account for three-quarters of Russia's single-family housing output. (For the views of executives on the high cost of construction in Russia, see the sidebar "Insider perspective: Thicker pipes and walls.")

Retail banking and Russia's financial system

The restructuring and resource reallocation needed throughout Russia's economy will be possible only with a comprehensive financial

Insider perspective: Thicker pipes and walls

Dmitry Konov
Chairman of the executive board and president of the petrochemical producer Sibur

The cost of construction for a petrochemical plant is 40 percent higher in Russia than in Europe. In China, it's 40 to 50 percent lower than in Europe. That's a twofold difference between Russia and China. Why is it more expensive in Russia? Lower productivity across the entire value creation chain, poor equipment quality, and the high cost of delivering this equipment from other countries, and lower-quality work that takes longer to do. It also appears that construction is more expensive because we have to use thicker pipes and thicker walls.

Vitaly Yakovlev
General director of the electric-power company Mosenergo

Dmitry hit the nail on the head about the width of pipes and walls. That immediately contributes to the cost of our power stations. Once, we didn't know certain procedures, and we actually had to redo them three times. Creative regulation—or, should I say, creative supervision—affects the entire process. And I would like to add an internal problem: we do not have the level of project management that is common in foreign companies.

infrastructure. To create one, the country needs credible rating agencies, better-developed financial instruments, and a bigger pool of long-term savings, as well as a banking sector that can pool domestic capital resources effectively and allocate them efficiently. Before the crisis, Russia had the world's fastest-growing retail-banking market, with risk-adjusted revenues expanding at a compound annual rate of 60 percent from 2000 to 2007.

Yet most of Russia's 1,000-plus banks lack the financial or physical scale to operate efficiently. The government could foster consolidation effectively by gradually tightening capital and reporting require-ments and risk-management standards—moves now being imple-mented with much caution. Restructuring of this sort would also increase productivity, now 23 percent of US levels after adjusting for differences in incomes and ten times lower when measured by physical transactions per employee.

Besides promoting such a restructuring, the government can also encourage higher productivity by curbing its regulation of the banks' branch-based transactions and cutting the bureaucracy involved in basic transaction processing. Meanwhile, the industry should cen-tralize back-office and administrative functions and work with utilities to expand the use of electronic bill payments and transfers.

Before the crisis, retail banking in Russia was growing faster than anywhere else in the world—but its low productivity (23 percent of the US level) leaves it vulnerable.

© Georges DeKeerle/
Getty Images
Moscow, Russia

Just consider a few facts. Russian banks must fill in large numbers of forms. One directive requires the regular submission of some 74 different reports to the central bank, compared with 1 report US banks submit every 15 days to the Federal Reserve System. Russian bank branches require up to three people, compared with one in the United States, to execute a single cash withdrawal. As a result, making a withdrawal, a deposit, or a payment from an account takes between two and five times as long as it does at US banks. Only about one-third of payment transactions in Russia are automated, compared with 70 percent in the United States and 90 percent in the Netherlands. Nonautomated transactions are on average 12 times more labor intensive than electronic ones.

Most banks haven't begun to centralize their back-office and administrative functions. To double the sector's productivity, the number of electronic payments must increase by 150 percent, and half of all payments will have to be undertaken outside bank branches. The experience of some local banks that have implemented productivity efforts suggests that these targets are quite achievable, with minimal capital investment.

The human dimension

Labor productivity improves only when work changes—because people undertake their current jobs more efficiently or move to other, more productive roles. To realize both possibilities, Russia must improve the way it educates and trains professionals and make it easier for workers to move around the economy and the country.

Labor skills

Despite high literacy rates and excellent technical education, Russia lacks key skills. By far the largest gaps, evident in all five sectors we studied, are in project management, largely as a result of 20 years of underinvestment and the resulting inexperience of managing large capital projects.

The electric-power sector also doesn't have enough people with plant design and construction know-how, and it is difficult to fill these gaps on a short-term basis by engaging engineers who have experience in construction contracting, since there are so few of them and the market is only emerging. In steel, even recent graduates tend to lack the project-management, teamwork, leadership, and foreign-language skills needed to oversee technological-modernization projects.

Upgrading outdated educational programs will help address this short-fall. Many design-management students in residential construction, for instance, still use equipment dating back to the 1950s. Topics such as designing to cost are often covered by antiquated curriculums. Adjusting them to global best-practice standards, as well as increasing the practical component in relevant courses, would raise skill levels throughout the economy.

Labor mobility

Russia can achieve its potential only if it promotes labor mobility among geographic regions and industry sectors. Historically, rapid per capita GDP growth has almost invariably been accompanied by such a shift in employment—first, from agriculture to manufacturing and, more recently, from manufacturing to financial, business, and trade services. In Russia, however, housing, infrastructure, legal, and cultural barriers hinder labor mobility.

Related articles on mckinseyquarterly.com

The power of productivity

How half the world shops: Apparel in Brazil, China, and India

Can Russian aerospace rise again?

Russia's federal and local governments, as well as its businesses, can facilitate the reallocation of labor by focusing on regional economic-development initiatives that create new jobs. Enhanced job-placement services and improved social programs will also help the country's workers become more mobile.

The restructuring of Europe's steel and automotive industries during the past two decades provides some guidance. From 1986 to 1996, 12 EU countries decreased employment in the steel sector by 200,000 people, a number roughly equivalent to the sector's excess employment in Russia. Likewise, during the 1990s a shift in automotive production to lower-cost countries led Volkswagen to shed 20 percent of the employees at its headquarters, in Wolfsburg, Germany. Virtually overnight, unemployment there soared to 18 percent. Five years later, thanks to a joint venture between the company and the municipal government, more than 11,000 new jobs had been created and the city's unemployment rate was 50 percent lower.

• • •

Russia's economy has made enormous strides over the past decade, but the forces behind its recent growth are weakening. By boosting productivity in the years ahead, the country can make its economy more competitive and improve the lives of its people. ○

The authors would like to thank Daria Bakatina, Jean-Pascal Duvieusart, Kevin Krogmann, and Jaana Remes for their contributions to the research underlying this article.

Copyright © 2009 McKinsey & Company. All rights reserved.

We welcome your comments on this article. Please send them to quarterly_comments@mckinsey.com.

Enduring Ideas

**Classic McKinsey frameworks that continue
to inform management thinking**

The three horizons of growth

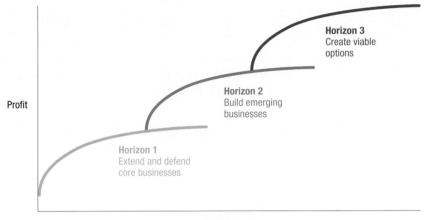

As companies mature, they often face declining growth as innovation gives way to inertia. In order to achieve consistent levels of growth throughout their corporate lifetimes, companies must attend to existing businesses while still considering areas they can grow in the future. The three-horizons framework—featured in *The Alchemy of Growth*[1]—provides a structure for companies to assess potential opportunities for growth without neglecting performance in the present.

Horizon one represents those core businesses most readily identified with the company name and those that provide the greatest profits and cash flow. Here the focus is on improving performance to maximize the remaining value. Horizon two encompasses emerging opportunities, including rising entrepreneurial ventures likely to generate substantial profits in the future but that could require considerable investment. Horizon three contains ideas for profitable growth down the road—for instance, small ventures such as research projects, pilot programs, or minority stakes in new businesses.

Time, as noted on the x-axis, should not be interpreted as a prompt for when to pay attention—now, later, or much later. Companies must manage businesses along all three horizons concurrently. Rather, it suggests the cycle by which businesses and ventures mature and move, over time, from horizon two to horizon one, or from horizon three to horizon two. The y-axis represents the growth in value that companies may achieve by attending to all three horizons simultaneously.

The framework continues to be useful, especially during uncertain times. The immediacy of concerns around horizon-one businesses can easily overwhelm other efforts important to the future of a company. C-suite leaders can use the three-horizons model as a blueprint for balancing attention to and investments in both current performance and opportunities for growth. O

[1] Mehrdad Baghai, Stephen Coley, and David White, *The Alchemy of Growth*, New York: Perseus Publishing, 1999.

Copyright © 2009
McKinsey & Company.
All rights reserved.

Artwork by Leigh Wells